ROUTLEDGE LIBRARY EDITIONS: CHRISTIANITY

Volume 9

CHRISTIANITY IN THE MAKING

CHRISTIANITY IN THE MAKING
A Critical and Historical Summary of the First Three Centuries

S. H. HOOKE

LONDON AND NEW YORK

This edition first published in 2021
by Routledge
2 Park Square, Milton Park, Abingdon, Oxon OX14 4RN

and by Routledge
52 Vanderbilt Avenue, New York, NY 10017

Routledge is an imprint of the Taylor & Francis Group, an informa business

First published 1926 Methuen & Co. Copyright 1926 S. H. Hooke

All rights reserved. No part of this book may be reprinted or reproduced or utilised in any form or by any electronic, mechanical, or other means, now known or hereafter invented, including photocopying and recording, or in any information storage or retrieval system, without permission in writing from the publishers.

Trademark notice: Product or corporate names may be trademarks or registered trademarks, and are used only for identification and explanation without intent to infringe.

British Library Cataloguing in Publication Data
A catalogue record for this book is available from the British Library

ISBN: 978-0-367-62307-4 (Set)
ISBN: 978-1-003-10879-5 (Set) (ebk)
ISBN: 978-0-367-62417-0 (Volume 9) (hbk)
ISBN: 978-0-367-63157-4 (Volume 9) (pbk)
ISBN: 978-1-003-10941-9 (Volume 9) (ebk)

Publisher's Note
The publisher has gone to great lengths to ensure the quality of this reprint but points out that some imperfections in the original copies may be apparent.

Disclaimer
The publisher has made every effort to trace copyright holders and would welcome correspondence from those they have been unable to trace.

CHRISTIANITY IN THE MAKING

A CRITICAL AND HISTORICAL SUMMARY OF THE FIRST THREE CENTURIES

BY

S. H. HOOKE
M.A. (OXON.) B.D. (LOND.)

METHUEN & CO. LTD.
36 ESSEX STREET W.C.
LONDON

First Published in 1926

PRINTED IN GREAT BRITAIN

CONTENTS

CHAPTER		PAGE
	PREFACE	ix
	INTRODUCTION	xi
	PROLOGUE — THE LIFE AND DEATH OF JESUS	1

PART I

THE GROUNDS FOR THE BELIEF IN THE RESURRECTION

I.	STATEMENT OF THE PROBLEMS	7
II.	GENERAL JEWISH BACKGROUND OF RESURRECTION BELIEFS	9
III.	SAYINGS OF JESUS RELATING TO BELIEF IN RESURRECTION	13
IV.	SAYINGS OF JESUS RELATING TO HIS OWN RESURRECTION	15
V.	PAUL'S BELIEF	20
VI.	THE EARLIEST CHRISTIAN PREACHING AND THE RESURRECTION	23
VII.	THE NATURE OF THE GOSPEL EVIDENCE FOR THE RESURRECTION OF JESUS	28
VIII.	THE ORIGINAL ENDING OF MARK	38
IX.	THE TWO TRADITIONS AND WHAT HAPPENED TO THEM	40

CHAPTER	PAGE
X. SUMMARY OF RESULTS	43
XI. THE DIVINE INTERVENTION VIEW	47

APPENDIX TO PART I

SYNOPTIC VIEW OF RESURRECTION NARRATIVES 62

PART II

THE RISE OF THE MOVEMENT IN JERUSALEM

I. THE MEANING OF PENTECOST	73
II. CHARACTERISTICS OF THE PRIMITIVE COMMUNITY	79
III. THE FIRST CRISIS AND ITS CAUSES	83

PART III

PAUL AND THE TRANSITION

I. PAUL IN ACTS	89
II. PAUL AND THE PRIMITIVE TRADITION	96
III. STATEMENT OF THE PROBLEMS	99
IV. PAUL AND THE SPIRIT	101
V. ADJUSTMENT TO THE NEW ENVIRONMENT	105

Contents

CHAPTER		PAGE
VI.	SALVATION AND ITS MEANING	108
VII.	GROWTH OF CHRISTOLOGY AND ORGANIZATION	112

PART IV

THE CHURCH IN THE EMPIRE

I.	MAIN CURRENTS OF INFLUENCE	119
II.	JESUS AND GOD	124
III.	THE FOURTH GOSPEL AND ITS INFLUENCE	127
IV.	THE EPISCOPATE AND ITS WORK	131
V.	THE COMPLETION OF THE CHRISTOLOGY	135
	EPILOGUE	139

APPENDICES

APPENDIX		
I.	PASSAGES FROM JEWISH APOCALYPTIC LITERATURE ILLUSTRATING BELIEFS CONCERNING THE RESURRECTION	143
II.	RABBINICAL ARGUMENTS FOR THE RESURRECTION	145
III.	THE THIRD DAY	147
	BIBLIOGRAPHY	149
	INDEX	151

PREFACE

IN a day of small books on great subjects it is hardly necessary to apologize for the contrast between the smallness of this book and the greatness of its subject. Whether the great historical phenomenon known as Christianity contains within it an immutable essence which renders it exempt from the processes of growth, change, and decay observable in other historical religions is a question which the slow movement of time will inexorably decide. This little book is simply an attempt to indicate the historical processes of birth, growth, and change observable in the first centuries of Christianity. The discussion of the inward spirit of Christianity has been deliberately avoided. The debt of such a book to other writers is necessarily too wide to be indicated in detail. But I should like to express my special indebtedness to my friend Canon Streeter, to whom all students of Christianity are immeasurably indebted, and to Professor Kirsopp Lake, whose admirable spirit of fairness and charity no attacks disturb. I should also wish to add that although I have used Professor Hogg's carefully reasoned argument for the supernatural element in Christianity as an example of the difficulties which that point of view presents to my own mind, yet I have nothing but admiration and esteem for his valuable work on the greatest of subjects.

LONDON
October, 1926
S. H. H.

INTRODUCTION

A SUFFICIENTLY long period of patient labour on the New Testament lies behind us to make it possible to take bearings on the position of modern thought to-day.

The main work of textual criticism has been done, and we possess with a fair degree of certainty the text of the early Christian documents as it existed about the time of the growth of the great creeds.

A group of scholars led by Dr. Sanday followed up the work of textual criticism by a long, patient study of what was called the Synoptic Problem. Their work, supplemented by that of many other students, established the main outlines of the growth of the Gospel tradition. While undoubtedly many points remain undetermined as yet, there is a general acceptance of the priority of Mark, of the existence of a separate source, or sources, of the teaching of Jesus, even earlier than Mark, of the dependence of " Matthew " and " Luke " upon these earlier sources, and of the late date and non-historical character of the Fourth Gospel.

These results produced a number of fresh studies of the life of Jesus and of the general historical background of his time. Along with these studies there appeared a number of very valuable investigations into special problems. Dr. Charles made the Jewish Apocalyptic literature available for students. Deissmann and other scholars threw fresh light upon the language of the New Testament and the broader significance of its vocabulary. Reitzenstein, Cumont, and other students of comparative religion brought under the notice of the general reader the importance of the mystery cults in the Roman Empire.

Fresh studies of later Jewish thought, the religion of the Synagogue and the growth of Rabbinical tradition began to appear, though this field is still waiting for a more thorough exploration. The point upon which these various lines of research converge to-day is the recognition that the early Christian historical work known as the Acts of the Apostles must be the next field of study.

It is now seen that further advance in the reconstruction of the Gospel tradition itself must wait on a fuller understanding of the conditions and point of view of the early community, Jewish at first, out of which the organization later called the Christian Church arose, and in whose midst the Gospels themselves had their origin. Several very significant studies have recently appeared. Dr. Harnack's shorter studies on the date of the Gospels and Acts, and on the book of Acts, together with his indispensable Mission and Expansion of Christianity, have been followed by Loisy's "Acts," Meyer's "Ursprung und Anfänge des Christentums," and the first two volumes of Jackson and Lake's much-abused but epoch-making commentary on Acts. It is beginning to be recognized that Acts presents similar problems in source-criticism to those of the Synoptic Gospels. An inversion of the generally accepted position is taking place. We no longer ask what is the relation of the early Church to the Gospels, but how did the Gospels arise out of the primitive community, how did it read and interpret the historical events constituting the life of Jesus? Apart from the documentary problems involved, three main historical problems emerge.

Introduction

The first is the most difficult, owing to the scarcity of evidence. It is the problem of how the movement which later became known as the Christian Church first arose in Jerusalem, or, in other words, what is the historical meaning of the event commonly called Pentecost?

The second problem is to explain the change from a purely Jewish community to a movement of cosmopolitan character.

The third is the problem of the transformation of a community with a narrow Jewish theology and a purely apocalyptic outlook into a world-wide organization with a definitely graded official hierarchy and a deep-rooted sacramental system.

Finally, any student who deals with these three problems with some degree of thoroughness comes to the insistent present-day problem of the relation of this historic organization to the changed world-outlook caused by the advance of modern science.

This book is an attempt to bring before students the existence of these problems, to induce them to read the documents of early Christianity afresh, and to indicate the main lines of approach to the reconstruction of the history of the early Church. The final problem, as always, is the conservation of values. Students of the life of Jesus have already discovered that honest search for the truth, while it may involve the pain of surrender of seemingly established values, yet in the end yields deeper and more firmly-established values.

The picture of one who cut his adventurous way through the barriers of ancestral prejudice and rooted religious customs, who loved greatly, who saw a vision of a new age, and died in loneliness and defeat to bring it about, has given to many a deeper meaning to life and a keener edge to the never-ending fight for advance than they could receive from the picture of the divine pre-existent person, foreknowing all, wielding omnipotence never so benevolently, and passing on to a foregone triumph.

In the same way those who approach this closely connected problem of the movement which arose out of the life of Jesus will undergo the same experience of loss and counterbalancing gain. However, Jesus himself with that realism that so strongly marked him, knew and said that people would always prefer old bottles and old wine. On that saying the history of the Christian Church is a perpetual commentary.

Before beginning this attempt to reconstruct in outline the main stages of the movement which resulted in Christianity, it has seemed necessary for the sake of completeness to give, first of all, a brief sketch of the career of Jesus of Nazareth, since it is at least clear that the movement in question arose from the impulse of the teaching, life, and death of Jesus.

S. H. H.

October 1926

CHRISTIANITY IN THE MAKING

PROLOGUE

THE LIFE AND DEATH OF JESUS

SOMEWHERE about the year A.D. 28 a religious movement arose in Galilee which attracted large numbers of the surrounding population. It began with the preaching of a man named John, whose message consisted of a denunciation of the unreality of contemporary Judaism, a call to repentance and an announcement of the near approach of judgment and the New Age of current apocalyptic expectation. Those who accepted the new prophet's warning were baptized by him in the Jordan. His movement probably went deeper and lasted longer than we should imagine. By Paul's time it had spread as far as Ephesus. Apollos of Alexandria was an adherent, and the Fourth Gospel shows that it was still a problem at the end of the first century.

Among the Galileans who came to hear the prophet's message was a young carpenter from Nazareth named Joshua, or, in its Greek form, Jesus. He was profoundly moved by the preaching of John, accepted baptism from him, and the whole course of his brief subsequent career is dominated by this experience.

At the moment of baptism he passed through a mystic experience, the account of which must have come from himself, though it has evidently been modified in transmission. The experience consisted of a vision followed by a period of conflict. For him the significance of the vision seems to have been that he was marked out by God for the central rôle in the establishment of the New Age, namely, that of the Messiah. The subsequent conflict turned on the obvious contrast between his own condition and the supernatural nature of the Messiah of current expectation. It turned also on the problem of the nature of his future course of action. There is clear evidence in the Synoptic Gospels that the mind of Jesus constantly went back to this experience as the determining point of his life.

The general direction given to the mind of Jesus by this experience seems to have been, first, a profound conviction that the movement begun by John was the first stage in the series of events destined to usher in the New Age; second, that his own part in the unfolding of the drama of the End was to carry on the work of John in his call to repentance and to await the time of God's intervention which would reveal him as the Messiah, the supernatural Son of Man.

There are strong grounds for believing that the passages in the Synoptic Gospels in which Jesus speaks of John as Elijah are part of the authentic tradition of his sayings. It seems that while the recorded sayings of Jesus undoubtedly reveal a mind of extraordinary moral penetration, fearlessness, and freedom from the religious tradition of his day, yet the drama of his life was shaped by the overmastering passion for the decisive change in the human order of things which was summed up in the phrase "the Kingdom of God." The belief in the reality and nearness of this

Prologue   3

event determined his interpretation of the events of his time, what he calls " the Signs of the times " ; it determined the course of his actions and furnished the reason for his final choice of death at Jerusalem.

The active part of his life was very brief. It cannot have been more than two and a half years, and may have been comprised in eighteen months. Apparently he accepted the imprisonment of John as a sign to himself to carry forward the work of John to completion. He began to preach in Galilee, and at the outset drew to himself a small group of followers, of whom the chief were Peter and the two sons of Zebedee, James and John. His preaching consisted of the call to repentance and the announcement of the New Age as close at hand. For him repentance—turning to God—went to the very springs of life and conduct ; it involved the turning from mere formal morality to a vital experience of the reality of God, and a willingness to stake everything with him on the reality of God's intervention.

The first period of activity in Galilee was brought to a close by a crisis. It is possible that Luke xiii. 31–33 gives the external cause of the crisis, namely, Herod's threat to kill Jesus if he did not leave Galilee at once. But this does not exclude the possibility that Herod's threat, following the execution of John, coincided with an internal crisis in the experience of Jesus. He did not merely leave Galilee because of Herod's threat, but because of a growing sense that some more drastic act was necessary, some mountain-moving act of faith that should make possible God's intervention and bring in the Kingdom. It is not accidental that his decision to leave Galilee coincides with the return of the Twelve. The return of the Twelve constitutes the focal point of the inner crisis, the sense that the first stage of his attempt had failed—repentance wide enough and deep enough had not been produced. It is impossible to ignore the significance of Jesus' passionate outbreak against the cities where his work had been done, "because they repented not." This does not mean that his following had decreased, or that a large body of adherents were not prepared to put him at their head and raise a revolt against Roman rule. This was not his aim, nor his conception of how the Kingdom should come. Hence Herod's threat only precipitated a course of action which he had already decided on.

Jesus determined to go up to Jerusalem. During the first stage of his activity there is no suggestion of the thought that his death would be necessary in order that the Kingdom might come But the crisis introduces this new and startling element into the Messianic conception. It was one which the disciples could not be expected to understand, and after the news had been broken to them at Cæsarea Philippi we can see in Peter's reaction the attitude of their minds to such a suggestion Hence there appears during the interval between the departure from Galilee and the arrival at Jerusalem an element of strain, a growing divergence between the mind of Jesus and the mind of the disciples. They were thinking of thrones and the realization of their dreams at Jerusalem. He was seeking to prepare their minds for a catastrophe. Between them and any realization of the dreams of a New Age lay a cross, a cup, a baptism. There was no thought in their minds of any profound moral issue to be faced, of any insuperable barrier to be surmounted, before the power of God could be liberated in action. But in his mind

Prologue

that was the overwhelming factor, a moral barrier of sin and unbelief to be broken through, certain ultimate conditions to be fulfilled, in order that God might be able to act. Elias had already come and suffered, the Son of Man must suffer likewise; he himself was called to give everything, leaving the issue to God. It seems clear that the issue turned for him upon resurrection. God would raise him and manifest him as Son of Man with power. While the form of particular sayings may have undergone modification in the light of subsequently developed beliefs about the resurrection, it seems to me certain that the belief that God would raise him formed a central element in Jesus' outlook.

When they arrived at Jerusalem events moved rapidly. Jesus joined issue with the Temple authorities on a point which touched them where they were most sensitive—their source of revenue from exchange and the sale of victims for the feasts. When they challenged his authority he faced them with John's movement, taking his stand upon that as the proof of God's activity among them. It was his ultimate ground of conviction. There are many problems connected with the last scenes which are still unsolved. But the attitude of Jesus stands out with startling clearness. On the one hand, he looks forward to the issue of his death. He believes that he will eat and drink again shortly with his disciples in the Kingdom of God. He promises to meet them in Galilee. Whatever the original words as he gave the bread and the cup at the supper may have been, they indicate at least his sense that everything turns upon this act of his own self-giving. Nothing can obliterate the certainty of his final answer to the high-priest as he closes the door of escape upon himself.

But, on the other hand, and in contrast with his profound conviction there is the evidence of a mortal struggle, a mental agony, showing that under the conviction there was the sense of possible failure. " If it be possible let this cup pass from me." This element was soon forgotten by the Church. It is obliterated in the Fourth Gospel, but it belongs to the original tradition. After the arrest the disciples scattered. Some of the women stayed to the end. The weakened body and mind strained to breaking point yielded rapidly and the usually long-drawn torment of crucifixion was soon over for him, so soon that later they thought it miraculous. But just before the end he broke the silence with the bitter cry that has come down through the centuries: " My God, my God, why hast thou forsaken me ? " How from this most heroic defeat arose a movement which shook the world is the question which we must go on to ask of history.

PART I

THE GROUNDS FOR THE BELIEF IN THE RESURRECTION

CHAPTER I

STATEMENT OF THE PROBLEMS

BETWEEN the brief drama of the life of Jesus of Nazareth and the long process of development which makes up the history of the Christian Church the common belief of that Church has placed an event, in Baron von Hügel's phrase, " a factual happening "—the Resurrection. Upon this event not only has the whole subsequent history turned, but it has furnished the key to the meaning of the universe and its order. Upon it may be said to rest the Christian view of Divine interposition in history and the Christian belief in the future life. It has often been said that the Resurrection of Christ is the crucial miracle; if that supreme act of Divine intervention is established other miracles offer no difficulty to faith.

Now it is at least clear that this event, like all other events in the life of Jesus and in the early history of the Christian movement, depends upon the evidence of the early Christian documents, and that evidence demands the same careful examination and the employment of the same principles of historical criticism which we give to any other group of events whose record is contained in contemporary documents. Before we can come to deal with the historical questions already mentioned, and especially the primary question of how the Christian movement started, it is absolutely necessary to deal historically with the grounds upon which the early Christian belief in the Resurrection of Jesus rested. In order to do this we have to inquire first of all into the beliefs about the Resurrection which were current in the time of Jesus. Secondly, we must examine the sayings of Jesus, which appear to refer to his own death and resurrection, in order to arrive at some conclusion as to his own attitude on this point. Thirdly, it is necessary to examine in detail the belief of the early Christian community prior to the formation and writing down of the Synoptic tradition. The evidence for this rests mainly upon Paul's letters, and upon the early narrative of Acts in so far as they represent primitive conditions. Fourthly, we must undertake the task, as far as limits of space will allow, of examining the evidence of the Synoptic Gospels and of the Fourth Gospel. Lastly, a brief discussion of what Professor Hogg calls "preternatural special providence" closes this first section of the book.

CHAPTER II

GENERAL JEWISH BACKGROUND OF RESURRECTION BELIEFS

IN the study of religious phenomena there is a distinction which is fundamental but which is very commonly unperceived. It is the distinction between the form and the content of a religious experience. For example, Joan of Arc was the subject of certain experiences, indubitably religious. These experiences culminated in visions and voices. The visions and the voices were attached in Joan's experience to St. Michael and St. Catharine. The names and forms of St. Michael and St. Catharine belonged to the form of Joan's experience. This form was due to certain traditional beliefs connected with these religious figures. But the reality of Joan's experience which is unquestioned is no guarantee of the validity and independent existence of St. Michael as the cause of her experience.

In the same way we have to make the distinction between the experience which underlay and gave impulse to the movement arising after the death of Jesus and the forms which it assumed. The two earliest forms which this experience took on, one of which has remained with little change as the central article of Christian belief, while the other has faded into the background of a loosely held expectation, were the belief in the resurrection of the body of Jesus and the belief in his immediate return as Messiah. The second belief was directly connected with the first and will be dealt with later on. The question to be answered first of all is whether the belief in the resurrection of certain classes of people as a special act of God existed in the minds of those who, as a result of their experience with Jesus, afterwards attached this belief to his person.

It is worth noting, in the first place, that in Paul's great exposition of the future state in 1 Cor. xv., he does not base the belief in the resurrection of the dead upon the fact of the resurrection of Jesus, but the reverse. He argues: " If the dead rise not, then is Christ not risen." To him the Resurrection of Jesus is a particular, though centrally important, case of an order of happenings which he already accepts on other grounds. The existing " form " of a belief in resurrection, not merely as a possible act of God, but as part of an accepted scheme of the future, made it easy for Paul to throw his special experience relating to Jesus into that form.

Paul, as an educated Pharisee, represents the general point of view of his order. We know from the New Testament and other sources that the Pharisaic point of view was not the only one prevalent in Jewish circles. Extra-canonical Jewish literature of the two centuries before Christ bears witness to the existence of a continually changing body of beliefs about the nature of the future Messianic Kingdom, the resurrection of the righteous, and the judgment connected with this Kingdom. Illustrative extracts from Jewish apocalyptic literature are given in an Appendix to this section of the book (see pp. 143-4).

The existence of a polemic against the resurrection such as is attributed to the school of Antigonus of

Socho is in itself a witness to the existence of the belief which it opposed.

Three general considerations should be noticed:

First, there is no question of the ability of God to raise the dead. The old Jewish stories of the raising of the dead by Elijah and Elisha are accepted without suspicion While the existence of Greek influence in sceptical doubts and questionings appears in the Talmud and in the Wisdom literature, yet in general the attitude of pious circles in Palestine is well expressed in Paul's words before Agrippa: " Why should you consider it incredible that God raises the dead ? "

Second, the belief in the resurrection of a particular class of people at a particular point in the future is the outcome of the struggle between Judaism and Hellenism in the second century B.C. The belief is really a fundamental element in Jewish theodicy of the time. The growing sense of failure and disappointment with the actual political condition of the Jewish people in Palestine as contrasted with the glowing promises of the prophets had given birth to the literature known as Apocalyptic. In this literature an increasingly sharp cleavage between " this age " and " the age to come " appears. The hopes of the faithful became more and more occupied with the age to come. This state of future blessedness and prosperity on earth would be the result of God's direct intervention. But the persecutions and martyrdoms which took place during the struggle with Hellenism created an acute problem which concerned the moral government of the world. The question of how the martyred righteous could share the blessings of the earthly Messianic Kingdom required an answer. The answer lay ready to hand in the existing belief in resurrection.

The only way in which God could justify himself was by raising these sufferers for the sake of the Law to enjoy their due portion in the Kingdom of the Messiah. Hence we find this belief has taken firm root in Jewish thought of the second century B.C.

Third, while the general outline of this group of beliefs underwent changes during the first century B.C., yet the New Testament itself is sufficient evidence for the persistence of this particular view-point up to and beyond the lifetime of Jesus. There is a most interesting example of the working of this kind of reasoning in Paul's first letter to the Christian community at Thessalonica. He had taught these people to believe in the near return of Jesus as Messiah to set up the kingdom of Jewish expectation. They had written to him concerning the problem of the fate of their believing relatives who had died before this speedily expected consummation. Paul's reply shows the working of this very tendency already mentioned. He argues that God will raise these dead believers at the return of Jesus as Messiah. Hence there can be no ground for doubting the existence of this " thought-form " of a resurrection as part of the general background of belief in the lifetime of Jesus and his contemporaries.

Various popular beliefs, such as the belief in Nero redivivus, the return of Arminius, of Frederick Barbarossa, the folk-myth of Drake's drum, and similar psychological phenomena have no direct relation to this particular problem of Jewish thought. It is primarily theological, although the existence of such an attitude amongst the Jewish common people, as elsewhere, is illustrated by the belief in the return of Elijah, and would naturally form suitable soil for the reception of such theological beliefs.

CHAPTER III

SAYINGS OF JESUS RELATING TO BELIEF IN RESURRECTION

THE next stage of our inquiry is concerned with the sayings of Jesus as recorded in the Synoptic Gospels. These sayings fall into two classes: those that refer to resurrection in general and those that refer to his own resurrection. There are two passages that belong to the first class:

(*a*) Matt. xii. 41, 42, Luke xi. 31, 32. In this saying the men of Nineveh and the Queen of Sheba are spoken of as rising in the day of judgment with the generation of Jesus to condemn them. The passage implies at the least a belief in a future judgment and in a resurrection connected with it. The genuineness of the saying has not been questioned.

(*b*) Matt. xxii. 23–33, Mark xii. 18–27, Luke xx. 27–40. This is the well-known dispute with the Sadducees, who presumably are aware that Jesus believes in the Pharisaic view of resurrection, and seek to turn it into ridicule. If we take the Marcan version of his reply, there are three points to be observed:

- (i) He refers to the Scriptures, implying that the general position of belief in the resurrection rests upon the Old Testament Scriptures.
- (ii) He refers to the power of God, i.e. presumably as exemplified in earlier cases of resurrection.

(iii) He uses a passage from the Torah in the familiar Rabbinical way to prove that the dead live with God.

The passage proves nothing as to the belief of Jesus regarding time or occasion of any special resurrection. It shows that He accepts the general view of resurrection and repudiates the grosser materialistic implications by which its opponents sought to turn it into ridicule.

A second appendix to this section contains illustrations from Rabbinical literature of the Rabbinical methods of defending this belief (pp 145-6).

From these two passages it would seem clear that Jesus accepted the general conception of resurrection as part of the plan of God for the future state. But they throw no light on the special problem of his belief as to the near approach of the " age to come " and the relation of his own death to that event. This brings us to the second class of passages.

CHAPTER IV

SAYINGS OF JESUS RELATING TO HIS OWN RESURRECTION

AS far as the text of the Synoptic Gospels is concerned there is no doubt of the existence of a number of sayings in which Jesus refers to his own death and resurrection. It is, however, impossible to take these sayings as they stand and make them the basis of a discussion of Jesus' attitude towards his own future. The genuineness of the sayings is part of the larger problem of the meaning of the life of Jesus. For those who accept the Four Gospels without criticism, and who regard the death and resurrection of Jesus as the central act of a divinely fore-ordained plan which Jesus knew from the beginning and which he foretold in these sayings, there is no problem. For those who accept the necessity of historical criticism of the Gospels there are, broadly speaking, two general positions in the light of which these sayings may be considered :

(i) There is the view which finds the historical Jesus to be an ethical teacher, a unique religious genius, far ahead of his own times. He had through his own experience arrived at the fundamental secret of life. He sought to impart this to others by example and teaching. He saw that death would be the ultimate issue of a life that diverged so widely from the accepted religious convictions of his time. He did not look for resurrection, but for the slow growth of the Kingdom of God after his death through the propagation of his secret by his followers. Hence he never uttered any predictions of resurrection, and the sayings which appear to foretell it really reflect the later belief of the first generation of his followers.

(ii) There is, on the other hand, the view that accepts the uniqueness of the ethical teaching of Jesus, but at the same time believes that he combined this with an apocalyptic world-view. That is to say, that he believed that the Kingdom of God would be the result of a divine act of intervention in the near future, and that his rôle in the Kingdom was that of the supernatural Son of Man. On this view it is possible to regard Jesus' attitude towards his own death as a conclusion to which he was forced by the logic of events, and that his sayings about his resurrection represent his belief, drawn from those contemporary beliefs of which we have spoken, that his entry into the Kingdom would be by means of a Divine act, that his resurrection would be the first act in his parousia, or manifestation as Son of Man.

Instead of regarding the difficult saying about the third day as the reflection of a later belief that his resurrection took place on the third day after his death, it is possible to reverse the process and regard the belief in the third day resurrection as a literal interpretation of a saying which originally rested upon an old Jewish interpretation of Hosea vi. 2. The grounds for this suggestion will be found in an appendix to this section (p. 147).

It is impossible here to discuss in detail the general reasons for this view of the life of Jesus. But the reader is referred to Schweitzer's "Quest of the Historical Jesus," the present writer's "Christ and the Kingdom of God," and Professor Cadman's very valuable little book "The Last Journey of Jesus to Jerusalem." Although Professor Cadman rejects the resurrection sayings on another ground, yet his book is a weighty defence of the apocalyptic view of the life of Jesus. This brings us to the third consideration mentioned in Part II of our first section, viz. the beliefs of the first generation of the Christian movement regarding the resurrection of Jesus, prior to the formation of the Gospel canon.

Note 1.

In Canon Streeter's recent book "The Four Gospels" the most important contribution to New Testament scholarship since the work of Westcott and Hort, the following significant passage occurs: "One reason why these erroneous assumptions have held sway so long is that the Synoptic Problem has been studied merely as a problem of literary criticism apart from a consideration of the historical conditions under which the Gospels were produced" (p. 229).

Synoptic criticism can provide no criterion for the authenticity of sayings or incidents peculiar to any one of the three Synoptic Gospels. Sayings such as, "Ye shall not have gone over the cities of Israel till the Son of Man be come," peculiar to Matthew, or "I am come to cast fire on the earth and what will I if it be already kindled," peculiar to Luke, incidents such as the resurrection of the saints in Matt. xxvii., or the trial of Jesus before Herod in

Luke xxiii., lie outside the province of Synoptic criticism as far as the question of their historical value is concerned. They have to be judged in the light of the more complex process of historical criticism.

Note 2.

Professor Cadman, in his most interesting and original little book " The Last Journey of Jesus to Jerusalem," while supporting in the main the apocalyptic view of Jesus' life, thinks that Jesus made no announcement of his resurrection. His reasons are summed up in the following passage : " Another element of the prediction which raises difficulties is the announcement of the resurrection. The Synoptic sources represent that our Lord conceived of His resurrection apart from His parousia. They were two distinct events separated by an interval of time, probably short but certainly real, and differently motived—the resurrection being a brief visit to personal adherents for their comfort and solace, the parousia being a return for judgment and the inauguration of His perpetual reign as ' The Son of Man.' But it is unlikely that our Lord ever drew this distinction between resurrection and parousia. His only return would be for judgment and the Kingdom, and then He would abide for ever with His own " (pp. 78-79).

Now I agree with Professor Cadman that Jesus probably made no distinction between his resurrection and parousia, but I do not see the grounds for his statement that the Synoptic Gospels make such a distinction.

It is only in the Fourth Gospel that the parousia is spoken of as a return to his own for solace and comfort. In the Synoptists three points appear : First, the manifestation of Jesus as Son of Man takes place after his death ; second, it will be shortly after his death ; thirdly, it will be connected with the establishment of the Kingdom on earth. The promise to meet them in Galilee does not conflict with these points for the setting up of the Kingdom must have a beginning and might well begin in Galilee. Hence it seems to me that if Jesus identified his resurrection with his parousia, as I think he did, there is no reason why he should not have announced it, at one time in resurrection terms and at another in terms of his manifestation.

CHAPTER V

PAUL'S BELIEF

THE two sources which we shall discuss as bearing on this question are the letters of Paul and the records of the early preaching in Acts. There are three points of view from which Paul treats of the resurrection of Jesus :

First, he deals with it as an historical event and incidentally gives grounds for his belief. Secondly, he regards it as the crucial event in the apocalyptic scheme. Thirdly, he deals with it as an event having important spiritual significance.

In Protestant theology the third aspect has been separated from Paul's main interest, which was apocalyptic, and has been made the basis of the most important part of the Protestant dogmatic scheme. The discussion of this, however, lies outside our present purpose.

The first two aspects were not sharply distinguished in Paul's mind, since for him the apocalyptic scheme was simply future history, so to speak, all human events being seen by him under the guise of that apocalyptic order.

In his fullest discussion of the subject in the fifteenth chapter of his first letter to the Corinthians we find first of all that he accepts the fact of the resurrection of the dead without question, and proceeds to deal with Greek sceptical difficulties in his own way. He takes the resurrection of Jesus in the first place as a particular case of the general belief. He alleges three

Paul's Belief

grounds for his belief in the particular historical event: First, it is "according to the scriptures"; secondly, it is a matter of contemporary belief which has been handed on to him (ὃ καὶ παρέλαβον); thirdly, it is a matter of personal experience (ὤφθη κἀμοί).

With regard to his first ground of belief, it is impossible to discuss it here, because he does not allege the particular scriptures in point. We shall, however, meet the question again in dealing with the early preaching in Acts.

His summary of contemporary tradition is only evidence for the existence at that time of the belief in a series of appearances of the risen Jesus. No details of the nature of the appearances are given, and it is impossible to relate the appearances mentioned to those described in the Gospels.

The only piece of first-hand evidence is his reference to his own experience, and concerning this he gives no details, nor does he elsewhere in his letter. In Acts, however, there are three accounts of this experience. One related by the author of the book, or by the compiler of the particular source of that section of the book, and the other two put into the mouth of Paul on two separate occasions. A comparison of the three accounts is an interesting study in the nature of historical evidence.

The two main questions concerning the nature of the evidence are those of what was seen and heard by Paul himself, and what was seen and heard by his companions. The three accounts vary and to some extent conflict, and only one point of agreement is found in the three, viz. that Paul saw a light. The words which he heard vary considerably, and in the account given to Agrippa become quite a long speech.

There is nothing in the evidence to show that Paul's

experience differed essentially from that, let us say, of Augustine with his " tolle, lege," or of Joan of Arc, Francis of Assisi, or any of the mystics whose visual and auditory experiences have been recorded. What was the actual cause and nature of Paul's experience is not relevant here. We are only concerned with the point that the narratives of Paul's experience provide no evidence of an external appearance of the risen Jesus. On the other hand, Paul's letters afford abundant evidence that the belief in the resurrection of Jesus was a fundamental and central element in the early Christian movement, and also that he himself shared that belief to the fullest extent. But Paul's emphasis is not on the material or physical side of the resurrection. He makes no mention of the empty grave, or of the physical proofs such as appear in later tradition, viz. the eating of food, the touching of the risen body, the stigmata, and so forth. For Paul the risen Christ is a " quickening spirit," to him the Spirit of Jesus, the Spirit of Christ, and the Spirit of God are equivalent terms. The resurrection of Jesus is for him the first act in the apocalyptic drama whose climax is the parousia of Christ, the raising of dead believers, and the establishment of the Kingdom. This climax is expected by Paul at first in his own lifetime. During the short interval the spirit of Christ is active in believers changing the elements of their mortal bodies with a view to their final transformation at the parousia.

The transformation of Paul's vivid, highly imaginative, realistic view of an apocalyptic world-order, in which the resurrection of Jesus is the central act, into a system of dogmatics is one of the strangest phenomena in the history of religious thought.

CHAPTER VI

THE EARLIEST CHRISTIAN PREACHING AND THE RESURRECTION

IT is unfortunate that the extant records of the earliest Christian preaching are so scanty. If, however, we may venture to take the records given in the early chapters of Acts as typical of the kind of preaching with which the movement in Jerusalem began, there are several interesting points which arise from these records. Leaving the question of source-criticism for discussion later on, we may for the present take the address given in Acts iii. as possibly the earliest specimen of public preaching in Jerusalem characteristic of the new movement. (iii. 20) Jesus is the servant of God, the God of the fathers, he is the predestined Messiah (τὸν προκεχειρισμένον Χριστόν). (iii. 18) He has been killed in fulfilment of prophecy. He has been raised by God, an historical fact of which the speakers claim to be witnesses. The Jewish audience is told that if they repent of their sin of ignorance in killing their Messiah he will at once return to set up the Kingdom (iii. 20) and fulfil the promises of the prophets (iii. 21).

This is a purely Jewish message whose point lies wholly in its apocalyptic outlook. The resurrection is not a mere proof of supernatural intervention in history, for the Jew needed no such proof, but it is a guarantee of the Messiahship of Jesus and of the speedy fulfilment of apocalyptic expectations.

There are strong grounds for supposing that the other record of the earliest preaching in Acts ii. is a doublet, a later version of the account in the third chapter. It shows evidence of the influence of the early Christian controversy with the Jews and its method, viz. the use of Old Testament prophets. Dr. Rendel Harris has thrown most valuable light on this almost unknown phase of the early development of Christianity in his book on "The Testimonies," to which the reader is referred.

In this passage the resurrection of Jesus is offered as a fulfilment of a proof-text, the passage in Psalm xvi., which is quoted in full from the LXX. Its main point turns on the Greek mistranslation of the Hebrew word שַׁחַת by διαφθορά, rendered in English by "corruption." The Hebrew word means "the pit," and the passage is the expression of the faith of the godly man that Jehovah will keep him from going down into Sheol, or the pit. No suggestion of resurrection is contained in the original. But the turn of the word "corruption" enables the early Christian apologist to use the passage as a prophecy of the resurrection of Jesus, and incidentally shows that physical resurrection is in question, "his flesh" does not " see corruption." This passage, together with the earlier passage from Joel in the same speech, are interesting examples of that use of the Old Testament as a storehouse of Christian proof-texts which is so characteristic of early Christian literature.

It is noteworthy that the emphasis does not lie on the proof of the resurrection, but on the identification through Hebrew prophecy of the risen Jesus of Nazareth with the Messiah. In the same connexion the Pentecostal phenomena are interpreted as the signs of the apocalyptic "day of the Lord," showing the same general apocalyptic outlook as the first passage already discussed.

The record of Stephen's speech contains no mention either of the resurrection or of the apocalyptic outlook. Peter's address to Cornelius and his friends in Acts x. shows clear traces of the point of view of the author of Luke xxiv. and Acts i. We have the beginning of the physical proofs, "who did eat and drink with him after he was risen from the dead" (x. 41), and the idea that the apostles were specially chosen to be witnesses of the resurrection (x. 41, cf. with i. 22).

The speech of Paul and Barnabas at Antioch, in Acts xiii., repeats the argument from Psalm xvi. that we found in Acts ii., and gives a brief summary (xiii. 28–31) of the Lucan account of the crucifixion, burial, and appearances. Paul's speeches, already discussed, complete the passages in Acts which purport to represent the early Christian preaching.

How far these speeches are genuine reports and independent of the growth of the Synoptic tradition is a matter for discussion. For a full examination of the question the reader may consult the article "Greek and Jewish Traditions of Writing History," by Henry Cadbury and the Editors, in Vol. II of Jackson and Lake's "The Beginnings of Christianity."

Two points directly related to our particular inquiry may be noted here:

First, it seems highly probable that the two reports given in Acts ii. and iii. are the only material in Acts referring to early beliefs in the resurrection of Jesus which are independent of the Gospel tradition.

Second, it is remarkable that they contain no details of appearances, or proofs of the historical fact of the resurrection of Jesus. They assume it, and represent a point of view which is either wholly occupied with the Messianic and apocalyptic significance of the resurrection or with the attempt to connect the resurrection with Old Testament prophecy.

Before we pass on to the examination of the Gospel tradition it may be worth while, for the sake of clearness, to sum up the main points so far resulting from our inquiry.

First of all, there is clear evidence for the existence of a belief among the Palestinian Jews in the time of Christ in resurrection as a general fact of Divine interposition, and in a special apocalyptic view of resurrection as part of the future order of events.

Second, there is evidence that Jesus shared in the general belief of his time in resurrection, and strong probability in favour of the view that he found a solution of his own particular problem in the belief in his own resurrection as the first act in the Divine drama of intervention upon which he staked everything. This particular element in his own belief was probably not understood or shared by his disciples.

Third, the earliest evidence shows the existence of a strong belief in the resurrection of Jesus among the early Jewish community in Jerusalem out of which the Christian Church arose. For the grounds of this belief among the original circle of Jesus' followers we are dependent entirely upon the Gospel narratives, which we shall next examine, since the evidence in Acts affords no grounds whatever for the belief, but merely proves that it existed. The only first-hand evidence from this material is Paul's. Examination of Paul's evidence elicits three main points: First, that Paul shared the general Pharisaic view of resurrection; second, that Paul had received the tradition of the resurrection of Jesus from the primitive Christian community and had worked it into his Pharisaic belief; third, that he had experienced a profound religious upheaval at a particular crisis in his life, but the narratives of this crisis afford no evidence for anything but a vision or spiritual experience. Paul's belief in the resurrection of Jesus must be considered as the product of the blending of these three factors if it is to be understood in true historical perspective.

CHAPTER VII

THE NATURE OF THE GOSPEL EVIDENCE FOR THE RESURRECTION OF JESUS

WE have found that in Paul's letters and in the source-material underlying our present book of Acts there exists a strong belief in the resurrection of Jesus, but the grounds for this belief remain so far unexplained. The existence of the resurrection of Jesus as an historical event is assumed, but not a particle of first-hand evidence from those who might have been eyewitnesses of the event is given in Acts. The nature of Paul's first-hand evidence has already been pointed out.

The only remaining source for the nature of the experience of the original group lies in the Gospels. Before examining the records of the burial and resurrection of Jesus given in the Gospels the following points need to be tested: First, we have no means of knowing what first-hand evidence, if any, underlies the Gospel records. In its present form all the evidence is second-hand. The earliest Gospel, Mark, according to very early Church tradition rests upon the reminiscences of Peter. It is impossible to establish the truth of this tradition. But, if it were true, the experience of Peter in regard to our particular point, the resurrection of Jesus, is by a strange documentary vicissitude entirely absent from Mark, as we shall see. Second, the remaining Gospels belong to a late period in the first century A.D., and so far from representing

The Nature of the Gospel Evidence 29

the original form of the tradition represent the form which that tradition had assumed after nearly a century of controversy and literary evolution. These facts must be borne in mind as we undertake a brief sketch of the evidence of the Gospels.

(A) MARK

The order of events following the death of Jesus is as follows: Joseph of Arimathea, a member of the Sanhedrin, asks for the body of Jesus and buries it in one of the rock-graves outside Jerusalem. The motive for his act is not given, unless the ἐπεὶ ἦν παρασκευή of xv. 42 be regarded as supplying it. The two Marys—Mary of Magdala and Mary the mother of James and Joses—are the only two witnesses of the burial. After the Sabbath is over they, together with Salome, buy unguents, and at sunrise on the first of the week they come to the grave to anoint the body. On the way they discuss the difficulty of removing the stone. Arriving at the place they find that the stone has been removed. They are alarmed by the sight of a young man in a white garment sitting at the right of the grave. He tells them not to be alarmed, says that Jesus is risen and that the grave is empty. He gives them a message for the disciples and Peter to the effect that Jesus will meet them in Galilee according to his promise. The women flee from the grave in a panic and say nothing of the episode to anyone. The narrative would have gone on to explain the reason for their silence but it breaks off in the middle of a sentence, ἐφοβοῦντο γάρ.

The fact that the earliest exemplars of Mark break off here, and that the remaining twelve verses are a much later addition, is now universally accepted. Full documentary evidence may be found in Swete's "Commentary" on the Gospel of Mark. The consequence is that the evidence of Mark goes no further than the facts above described. There is no evidence contained there for any appearance of Jesus.

The significant points in the fragment are the reference to a meeting in Galilee, and the silence of the women. What Mark would have gone on to relate is a matter for conjecture, and we shall see later that there are grounds for reasonable surmise concerning the contents of the lost ending of the gospel.

(B) MATTHEW

When we compare Matthew and Luke with Mark it is obvious that as in the main body of the Gospels so in the narrative of the burial and resurrection the compilers of these two gospels have used Mark as their groundwork. It is also possible that they possessed Mark in an unmutilated form. But it is also clear that both of them depend on other traditions beside Mark In examining the narratives of Matthew and Luke three points call for special attention :

First, the way in which Matthew and Luke use Mark.

Second, the nature of the traditions which they blend with the Marcan narrative.

Third, the reasons for their changes and additions. Matthew's account shows the following changes and additions as compared with Mark :

Joseph is a rich disciple of Jesus. His membership of the Sanhedrin is dropped. A strange fragment of tradition is inserted by Matthew to the effect that

The Nature of the Gospel Evidence 31

after the death of Jesus many graves were opened by the earthquake, and the bodies of " Saints " who had died arose and appeared to many in Jerusalem. Merely from the historical point of view the silence of Acts concerning so startling an event is significant.

The grave is a private grave belonging to Joseph. The two Marys watch the burial. Matthew inserts another tradition, viz. the story of the setting of a watch over the grave. This story implies that the Jewish authorities knew of a resurrection prediction. It also implies a controversy between Jews and Christians concerning the resurrection, with charges of fraud on both sides, which is entirely absent from the early narrative of Acts.

The two Marys come on the first of the week, not to anoint the body, but to watch the grave, suggesting resurrection expectations not found in Mark.

The young man of Mark becomes an angel who descends from Heaven, rolls away the stone, and sits on it. The watchers become " as dead men." The angel gives substantially the same message to the women as the young man in Mark, with the omission of Peter's name.

As in Mark the women run from the grave, but joy is coupled with their fear, and instead of the silence of Mark they go to carry word to the disciples. On their way they meet Jesus, whom they hold by the feet and worship. He repeats the message of the young man in Mark concerning the meeting in Galilee.

Here Matthew inserts the remainder of the story of the watch and the Jerusalem authorities. Then without relating any meeting between the women and the disciples he tells us that the eleven disciples went to Galilee, met Jesus by appointment on a mountain, and received a charge from him to disciple all nations and to baptize them in the Triune name. There is no account of any ascent into Heaven.

It is probable that Matthew's account of the appearance of the risen Jesus to the disciples in Galilee may represent some part of the lost end of Mark, since the author of that gospel apparently intended to relate the fulfilment of the young man's message to the women, already anticipated by the words of Jesus at the Supper (Mark xiv. 28).

Hence both Mark and Matthew adhere to the tradition that the experience which convinced the disciples that Jesus was risen took place in Galilee.

(C) LUKE

When we come to Luke we find very significant changes. While the narrative of Mark is followed up to the account of the visit of the women to the grave, the author entirely abandons it from that point. There are minor points of difference in the account of the burial for which the reader may refer to the Synoptic table appended to this section. But from the visit of the women to the grave onward the divergence of Luke's account is complete. The women see two angels at the grave, who give them a message which is clearly a paraphrase of the message in Mark. The injunction in Mark to tell the disciples to meet Jesus in Galilee is changed into a reminder of Jesus' prediction in Galilee that he must die and rise again. The women carry the message of the empty grave to the disciples and the rest in Jerusalem, who disbelieve their report. The Western text inserts a brief account of Peter's visit to the grave and of his finding the grave-clothes (xxiv. 12).

The Nature of the Gospel Evidence

There is no appearance of Jesus to the women: indeed, it is denied by implication (xxiv. 23).

Then follows the account of the first appearance, viz. to the two on the way to Emmaus, on the evening of the first day of the week. The two return to Jerusalem at once with the news of their experience and find the disciples already discussing the news of an appearance to Peter of which no account is given anywhere. At this point Jesus appears to the group, establishes his physical existence by eating in their presence, proves to them that His death and resurrection are the fulfilment of Old Testament prophecy, and charges them to remain at Jerusalem until they receive power from on high. A world-wide mission is also indicated.

Then, apparently still on the same evening, Jesus leads the group out to Bethany, blesses them, and is carried up to Heaven. (The Western text omits the words " and was carried up to Heaven," and " they worshipped him.") The disciples return to Jerusalem and remain there in daily attendance at the temple.

It is at once obvious that Luke is following here a tradition which is quite irreconcilable with the tradition of Mark and Matthew. According to this tradition there is no flight to Galilee and no appearance of Jesus in Galilee. Everything happens in Jerusalem or its immediate neighbourhood, and apparently on one day, the first of the week. Luke expressly leaves no loophole for a visit of the disciples to Galilee, since they remain in Jerusalem till Pentecost.

Hence the comparison of the Synoptic Gospels makes clear the main point which we are now concerned with, that there existed at the time of the compilation of the Gospels two distinct and incompatible traditions, the first placing the scene of the appearance of Jesus to the disciples in Galilee, the second entirely in Jerusalem.

The relative value of these two traditions will be discussed when we have examined the rest of the evidence that is available.

(D) ACTS

Acts i. contains certain material which calls for examination before we go on to the Fourth Gospel. It is generally conceded that the Third Gospel and the book called Acts are from the same hand, forming the parts of a connected historical work.

In the first eleven verses of Acts i. a slightly different account is given from that contained in Luke xxiv. Jesus is said to have spent a period of forty days with the disciples after his resurrection, and finally to have ascended in a cloud to Heaven from the Mount of Olives. Two angels then announce his return to the disciples.

This somewhat divergent tradition, nevertheless, confirms the main point that Jerusalem was the only scene of Jesus' resurrection activities, in the view of the author of Luke and Acts.

(E) JOHN

The variations and additions found in the Johannine narrative of the passion and resurrection are numerous and striking. As in the case of other material in the Gospel they raise the difficult question of the historicity of the whole story. It is not possible to discuss so large an issue here. The main point that concerns us in our present inquiry is that the author of the Fourth

The Nature of the Gospel Evidence 35

Gospel knows the earlier accounts of the Synoptists and has his own reasons for departing from them.

The outline of his story of the burial and resurrection is as follows: Although the mother of Jesus and " the disciple whom Jesus loved " are present at the end, it is still Joseph of Arimathea who claims the body. Joseph is a secret disciple. Nicodemus is associated with him in the burial. The presence of the women at the grave is not mentioned. Mary of Magdala comes alone early on the first of the week to the grave, it is not said for what purpose. She sees the stone removed, assumes that the body has been taken away, and comes to tell Peter and " the other disciple." These two run to the grave, find it empty, but are convinced by the disposition of the clothes that Jesus is risen. The words in xx. 8, " he saw and believed," can hardly mean anything else, especially as the contrast seems suggested by the next verse with proof from the Scriptures. They return home, but Mary, who has apparently come back to the grave, remains there weeping. She sees two angels sitting in the grave, who ask why she weeps. Turning from them she sees a man whom she supposes to be the gardener but immediately recognizes as Jesus. He forbids her to touch him, because his ascension has not yet taken place, but sends her to the disciples with the message that he is about to ascend to the Father. She delivers the message.

On the evening of that day we have the appearance, which is parallel to that in Luke xxiv, 36-49. Jesus appears suddenly in the room whose doors are closed, shows his hands and side, and gives the Spirit to the disciples by breathing on them. There is no mention of eating, as in Luke, and the number of disciples present is not given.

Finally, in an epilogue, we have the account of an appearance (μετὰ ταῦτα, "after these things") to seven disciples by the sea of Galilee. There is a miraculous draught of fishes (cf. Luke v. 1-11); Jesus, standing on the shore, is recognized by the beloved disciple. The disciples, on landing, find that a meal has been prepared for them by Jesus. Afterwards follows the threefold question to Peter, "Lovest thou me?" the prediction of Peter's death, and the announcement that the beloved disciple is to tarry till the return of Jesus.

It is quite impossible to reconcile this story, as an historical narrative, with the Synoptic traditions, but the moment we approach it as an allegorical interpretation of the spiritual relation between Jesus and the early Church, a spiritualization of the literal details of earlier traditions, it opens up a very interesting and fertile field of thought. However, for the purpose of our inquiry there are two main points to be noticed:

First, the Fourth Gospel is evidence for the existence, at the time of its final editing of the two traditions, the Galilean and the Jerusalem tradition. Unlike Luke, the redactor does not ignore the inconvenient Galilean tradition, but endeavours to blend it with the Jerusalem tradition.

Second, the comparison of the story told in Luke v. 1-11, with the account of the appearance in John xxi., possibly supported by the tradition underlying the Apocryphal Gospel of Peter, affords a basis for reconstructing the general outline of the lost ending of Mark. We shall return to this point again in the last chapter of this section.

(F) The Last Twelve Verses of Mark

Examination of this fragment shows, first, from the evidence of style, that it is not by the author of the Gospel, and second, from its contents that it is a condensed summary of the appearances related in Luke and John. Here it adds nothing to the evidence, and is only of interest as showing that the need was felt of replacing the original end of Mark by a conclusion which was in agreement with the Jerusalem tradition.

(G) The Apocryphal Gospel of Peter

A fragment of this gospel, which is mentioned by Eusebius, was discovered in 1886. It contains a narrative of the passion, burial, and resurrection of Jesus. Its probable date is early in the second century. The fragment was edited by Professor H. B. Swete, and has also been reprinted by Professor Kirsopp Lake in his book, "The Historical Evidence for the Resurrection of Jesus Christ."

The value of the fragment lies mainly in the fact that it appears to be an independent witness to the existence of the Galilean tradition. The fragment breaks off with an account of the return of Peter, Andrew, and Levi, and possibly others, to the sea of Galilee after the crucifixion.

The balance of probability seems against the dependence of this fragment on the Fourth Gospel, although the use of Mark and Matthew seems clear.

CHAPTER VIII

THE ORIGINAL ENDING OF MARK

BEFORE discussing the total evidence of the Gospels which has been thus briefly summarized the question of the original ending of Mark may be touched on.

The account of Mark, as far as it goes, suggests the scattering of the disciples and the intention to relate an appearance or appearances to them in Galilee.

In Luke v. 1-11 we have an account of the call of Peter, James, and John which differs widely from that given in Matthew and Mark, and also closely resembles the story related in John xxi.

Now while it is possible that John xxi. is an amplified version of the tradition of the call of the first disciples represented by Luke v. 1-11, it is still more probable that Luke v. 1-11 represents an incident belonging to the tradition of the Galilean resurrection-appearance which Luke, who had no room for the Galilean tradition, has transferred to the beginning of the ministry.

The story of Peter's experience expressed in the words, "Depart from me, for I am a sinful man, O Lord!" is far more intelligible if it is related to Peter's remorse at his denial suggested by the incident in John xxi.

It is also generally recognized that the last chapter of John does not form part of the original plan of the Fourth Gospel. Hence it would seem that it existed as a separate fragment of tradition which the final

The Original Ending of Mark

editor of the Fourth Gospel thought too valuable to reject and has embodied in an epilogue.

The suggestion is that Luke v. 1-11, John xxi., and the account in the Gospel of Peter of the return of Peter and his companions to the Sea of Galilee, represent three distinct fragments of the original ending of Mark and consequently of the earliest form of the Galilean tradition.

CHAPTER IX

THE TWO TRADITIONS AND WHAT HAPPENED TO THEM

THE outstanding result of an examination of the Gospel evidence for the resurrection of Jesus is the existence of two streams of tradition which cannot in any way be reconciled. The earlier tradition represents the original resurrection-appearance as taking place in Galilee. The disciples are scattered after the arrest, or possibly after the crucifixion, they return to Galilee to their fishing, and are there convinced of the resurrection of Jesus.

The later tradition places the whole series of experiences in Jerusalem. There is no break between the visit of the women to the grave and the Ascension. Everything happens in Jerusalem or its immediate neighbourhood, and the disciples remain in Jerusalem until Pentecost and the beginning of the new movement.

Which of these two traditions represents the historical order of events is in the last resort a matter of intrinsic probability. It is obvious that to Luke and his generation everything centred in Jerusalem, the movement appeared to have its rise there, it was the mother-church. But there is no motive apparent for the rise and persistence of the Galilean tradition.

It is, however, not difficult to see in the mutilation of Mark, and in Luke's transformation of those details of Mark which point to a Galilean appearance, the

The Two Traditions 41

gradual obliteration of a tradition whose source was forgotten in the subsequent centring of interest in Jerusalem.

Hence intrinsic probability seems to point to the Galilean tradition, now half-obliterated by the later Jerusalem tradition, as the original narrative of the events immediately following the death of Jesus.

If this is the case it becomes necessary to explain how the story of the women's visit to the grave entered the stream of tradition, since the disciples, according to Mark, have fled to Galilee, while the women remain in Jerusalem. Further, and in complete contradiction to Matthew and Luke, Mark says that the women said nothing about their experience.

It also becomes necessary to explain other elements in the later tradition—the angels, the watch at the grave, the visit of the disciples to the grave, and the appearances on the way to Emmaus and at Jerusalem.

It is possible to trace certain tendencies at work which have produced from the original account as far as we can reconstruct it the additions and modifications which have yielded the varying forms of narrative embodied in the Gospels and Acts. We have first the Jerusalem tendency. Through the influence of the belief that Jerusalem alone had been the scene of the events which led to the beginning of the Christian movement the original account of the Galilean experience was changed. The women's adventure at the grave was joined to later experiences of various groups of disciples at Jerusalem, and rounded off by the account of the ascension in such a way as to give a connected account of experiences happening entirely in Jerusalem, and leaving no room for any return to Galilee.

Then we have the Jewish controversy tendency. The narratives were modified and expanded in such a way as to reflect the course of controversy between the Jews and the primitive Church. The story of the rent veil, the watch at the grave, and the discourses of Jesus after the resurrection proving the necessity of his death and resurrection from the Old Testament, illustrate this tendency at work.

Then we have the dogmatic tendency, that is, the tendency to modify the story in the interests of certain doctrinal beliefs about Jesus which grew up under the stress of early doctrinal controversy.

The special stress on the empty grave, the touching of the resurrection body, the stress on the fact that the risen Jesus ate food before the disciples, reflect the insistence on his corporeity as against the views of the Docetists. The command to baptize and the introduction of the Trinitarian formula in Matthew probably represent a similar dogmatic tendency.

Lastly, under the influence of the apocalyptic and supernatural point of view of the time the young man of Mark becomes the angel of Matthew, two angels in Luke and Acts. We have the story of the risen saints in Matthew, connected with the growth of the later belief in Christ's preaching to the dead, and the mediaeval legend of the Harrowing of Hell.

Possibly the idea of the Ascension is due to the same cause.

CHAPTER X

SUMMARY OF RESULTS

BEFORE we attempt a final summing up of the results of the application of historical criticism to the narratives of the resurrection there are two considerations worth pointing out :

First, it will probably surprise anyone who attempts a critical study like this for the first time to find how slender and confused is the basis of evidence for the physical facts, as they are assumed to be, upon which so imposing a structure has been built.

Secondly, anyone who studies the earliest Christian literature will be struck by the slight emphasis laid on the historical and factual side of the growing Christian faith. If we had nothing but Paul's letters as our source we should know nothing of the life of Jesus at all, we should not know that he had ever wrought a miracle, we should only know that he was crucified, buried, and raised, and incidentally that he ate the Last Supper with his disciples.

Paul is only interested in a Christ who belongs to a non-historical spiritual order of happenings, a risen, quickening, and returning supernatural person.

This emphasis persists through the first three centuries, side by side with the growth of interest in the historical Jesus ; and we find Origen, in his famous division of Christians into somatic, psychic, and pneumatic stages of growth, giving the highest place to the man who has completely transcended the historical Christ.

People had come to believe that Jesus was the Messiah, Servant of God, Son of God, the Second Person in the Trinity, Judge of Men, and Saviour of Men, before the desire to know more of the historical facts concerning him gave rise to the growth of the Gospels.

Hence the historical facts, especially those relating to such parts of his life as were most important for these doctrinal beliefs, were liable to be interpreted and transmitted under the influence of these beliefs.

This is the fundamental fact to be recognized to-day in the study of the records of early Christianity.

Returning, then, to the summary of results :

First, while it is probable that Jesus did look forward to his own resurrection as the Divine means of bringing about his coming and manifestation as Son of Man, it is very improbable that his followers understood this part of his outlook. At the same time, sayings which they could not understand, indeed did not wish to understand, at the time of his uttering them, may have remained in their minds and returned later on to influence and reinforce their beliefs.

Second, it is certain that a general belief in the resurrection as an act of God, both in the past and as an element of the future order of events, had a firm hold on the popular mind at the period with which we are dealing. This would make it natural and inevitable that the experiences of the disciples and of Paul after the death of Jesus should take the form of this belief, and that it should become more and more sharply defined as a physical event.

Third, the earliest tradition seems to suggest the

Summary of Results

following possible reconstruction of the actual course of events : Immediately after the arrest of Jesus those disciples whose home was in Galilee scattered and made their way back to Galilee and there tried to pick up the broken threads of life and the old occupations. Some of the women remained in Jerusalem. Through a series of incidents, capable perhaps of a supernatural interpretation, such as the story of the draught of fishes, the disciples in Galilee came to the conviction that Jesus was still alive. Their memories of him, the depth of the impression which his personality had made upon them, the strength of the hope with which he had inspired them—these elements, temporarily submerged by the shock of his arrest and death, awoke in them and possibly produced in various members of the group similar experiences to those of Paul. They became convinced in Galilee that Jesus was still alive. Their belief took the only form which it could take in that age, reinforced, it may be, by the memory of his own sayings, and finally brought them to the point of the determination to return to Jerusalem in spite of the risk and there find occasion to carry on the mission of Jesus, the announcing and establishment of the Kingdom of God.

What happened in Jerusalem carries us into Acts, where the same process of criticism and reconstruction is necessary. But this much may be said here in connexion with the Jerusalem resurrection tradition. The return of the disciples to Jerusalem is part of the Galilean tradition which has been obliterated by the Jerusalem story, according to which they never returned to Galilee. But we shall see in Acts the possible point of junction. On their return, without definite plans, they meet the women and hear for the first time the story of their experience at the grave. Other experiences follow which later on formed the basis for the Jerusalem story which Luke has adopted. We can now pass on to the examination of the opening chapters of Acts, but before doing so I have ventured to turn aside from the historical inquiry to discuss briefly certain issues arising from the supernatural, or preternatural (to use Professor Hogg's word), view of the resurrection.

It is impossible to do more than suggest certain conclusions arising from this view and certain difficulties which it seems to present to the modern mind.

The next chapter may be treated as an appendix and omitted for the present by those who wish to carry on the historical discussion without a break.

CHAPTER XI

THE DIVINE INTERVENTION VIEW

THE author of the Epistle to the Hebrews in a single sentence describes the attitude of his time towards the course of events constituting the beginning of Christianity. He speaks of those who participated in the Christian movement as having "tasted of *the powers of the age to come.*" As this point of view dominated the first historians of the movement and has continued to dominate its interpreters ever since, it seems necessary to examine the implications of such a point of view.

Both Jesus and the pioneers of the movement which afterwards became known as Christian believed, first, that the general course of events in which they played a part was divinely determined and was about to culminate in "the age to come," a new order in which the will of God would be realized on earth as it had never been before. Secondly, they believed that certain events arising within their experience were evidences of the special working of the power of God pointing to the reality of the new age and directed to its establishment.

Professor Hogg, in his recent book "Redemption from this World," has given what is probably the ablest defence of the "miraculous" interpretation of the history which we are studying that has yet appeared in English.

He has stated this position so admirably that in

outlining his statement it seems clear that we are not dealing with a man of straw, put up to be demolished, but with a modern, carefully-reasoned defence of the whole " miraculous " point of view.

First of all, interpreting the attitude of Jesus in modern terms, Professor Hogg thinks that "within the phenomenal or created universe, which in its completeness—if *per impossibile* it ever could be completed—would be the exhaustive self-manifestation of God, there is a partially isolated realm which very inadequately displays his wealth of resource and benevolence of purpose, and the miraculous or supernatural involves the irruption into this realm of some of the reserves of cosmic energy which do not ordinarily have free operation there." The "isolated realm" here spoken of is elsewhere described as the portion of experience which science has succeeded in describing in terms of " natural law."

"Contraventions," says Professor Hogg, "of seemingly established scientific laws are nothing but interferences, on the part of the real cosmic order, with the success of our theory of that order in passing itself off as practically adequate."

Secondly, Professor Hogg goes on to say : " Now and again there occur events, the perfectly unique appropriateness of which to the peculiar needs of some individual human situation seems to leap to the eye. This recognition of a unique appropriateness is a matter of intuition ; it is neither helped nor hindered by the degree in which we are able to discern in the event an exemplification of general laws. No matter how many be the laws to which such an event conforms, we realize intuitively that it was not for the sake of such conformity, but for its own sake, or to render its

The Divine Intervention View

own uniquely individual service, that the event took place."

Professor Hogg thinks that this intuitive apprehension of events is superior to scientific or generalized apprehension; it is " less unlike the manner in which God apprehends them when He wills them."

Events capable of being thus apprehended he describes as " special providences." " A miracle is a ' special providence ' in which we not only fail to discern an exemplification of general laws, but perceive the very opposite; it is a ' special providence ' in which we perceive a contravention of what our best knowledge has hitherto taken to be laws of the cosmic or universal order. We describe as miraculous or religiously supernatural whatever impresses us as at once a ' special providence ' and a preternatural phenomenon."

Thirdly, Professor Hogg thinks that the phenomena which he thus describes depend upon faith in the redemptive purpose of God, that " the subtle texture of the cosmic order must be shot through with potencies which only the touch of filial fingers can evoke, and which only a spirit of confiding trust and eager loyalty is competent to direct."

Lastly, and expressing his fundamental postulate, Professor Hogg says : " The author must crave liberty here to take for granted the religious and philosophical position that a Divine Heavenly Father is the ultimate meaning of everything that is real."

To follow the full course of Professor Hogg's careful philosophical argument the reader should in fairness study the book itself, and whether he agrees with its ultimate position or not he cannot fail to find it most stimulating and suggestive.

I only wish to point out here certain difficulties in this statement of the "miraculous" view of the beginning of the Christian movement.

First of all, it is admitted that the "enclave," to use Professor Hogg's word, which constitutes the sphere of natural law very inadequately displays God's wealth of resource and benevolence of purpose. Hence apart from the philosophical grounds upon which the existence of the Divine Heavenly Father may depend, grounds which Professor Hogg for reasons of space does not discuss, such an existence of benevolent and redemptive purpose must depend almost entirely on the irruption into the sphere of natural law of these reserves of cosmic energy of which Professor Hogg speaks. Here arise two points for consideration.

First, since "natural law" means nothing more than the observed regularity in the behaviour of things, there is no attempt on the part of science in general (although there may be scientific dogmatists as there are theological dogmatists) to pass off this provisional charting of an observed order for anything more than it is—a tentative, groping, ever-advancing comprehension of how the universe works. But the question arises whether, as fresh portions of the uncharted cosmic energy which Professor Hogg speaks of are brought within this comprehension of order, they cease to bear that special aspect of benevolent purpose which they seem to bear as "irruptions." And further, since the final end of this purpose would seem to be the complete removal of the barrier between the "enclave," which constitutes the domain of natural law, and the reservoir of cosmic energy, it is not clear what will happen either to the domain of natural law,

The Divine Intervention View

or to the reservoir when it has completely overflowed the "enclave."

Secondly, since the irruption of cosmic energy consists of redemptive beneficent acts or events, these events cannot escape the scrutiny of another science, which, though it may not claim the mathematical exactness of the physical sciences, is none the less a science in its own right, history.

Here I find a very serious difficulty, for the whole claim of a beneficent irruption rests upon the value of evidence. But when the nature of the evidence is examined we find a number of considerations which make us at least hesitant in accepting it as proof of the particular point at issue.

The grounds for the belief in the beneficent irruption of cosmic energy consist in a large body of events, some national, such as battles, epidemics, disturbances of the course of nature, some personal, such as deliverances from danger, divine messages, and so forth, which belong almost entirely to Jewish and early Christian history, for the accounts of similar events in early Babylonian, Greek, or Roman history are not usually taken into account as evidence for the irruption in question. But as soon as this body of events is examined historically a considerable shrinkage takes place.

It is recognized that many stories which pious minds have taken literally were never intended by their authors as other than allegories. Nations have always tended to regard victories as evidences of Divine favour and interposition on their behalf, and in the same way to regard famines and pestilences as Divine acts. But it will suffice at present, since space will not allow a discussion of the whole development of the idea of God and of the particular conception of his intervention in human affairs connected with that idea, to examine the smaller body of evidence limited to the experience of Jesus, since Professor Hogg's argument is entirely based on this.

Here it is necessary to make certain points clear.

First the real crux of the position does not lie in the general argument for the possibility of events which contravene or seem to contravene natural laws. That possibility is freely admitted. At any time discoveries such as the properties of radium may compel the readjustment of views concerning the order of nature. The real crux lies in the nature of the historical evidence for the events which are said to contravene natural laws.

Now, whether we call them " powers of the age to come," or not, there is no question but that the life of Jesus was marked by exhibitions of a power which both he and his contemporaries regarded as the action of God.

Nevertheless, this admission does not absolve us from the necessity of a careful critical examination of the evidence for these exhibitions of power.

A particular case will illustrate several of the points at issue in this discussion.

An incident in the last week of Jesus' life is related in Matthew and Mark as an example of supernatural action. As told in Matthew, Jesus returning to Jerusalem from Bethany, early in the morning, saw a fig-tree by the way, and in the hope of finding some of the dried-up fruit of the previous year upon it, came up to it. He found nothing, " cursed it," and before the eyes of his astonished disciples it withered instantly. The conversation which followed shows that both

The Divine Intervention View 53

Jesus and his disciples regarded the occurrence as a Divine act.

But when we compare Mark with Matthew we discover that the story has been modified in transmission. As Mark told the story a period of twenty-four hours elapsed between the words of Jesus concerning the fig-tree and the observation by Peter next morning that the fig-tree had withered.

Hence there was time enough for natural causes to operate. But, even so, the story illustrates the second point quoted from Professor Hogg's argument, namely, the intuitive apprehension of the unique appropriateness of an occurrence to an individual situation. Jesus apprehends the unique appropriateness of the withered fig-tree to his individual situation and regards it as an act of God.

Now I am not prepared to admit that this is intuition. It is inference from a major premise. Assuming the existence of a beneficent Father on general grounds I argue that this particular occurrence, because it is appropriate to my individual situation, is a case of the Father's beneficent intervention. Then the occurrence becomes evidence for the irruption of beneficent cosmic energy into the domain which so inadequately displays that beneficence. It seems clear that a great deal of what is called evidence depends upon this "intuitive apprehension" of the appropriateness of events to individual situations.

In this way many events which in other respects fall within the domain of natural law are capable of being interpreted as "special providences." As a religious point of view based on a certain fundamental postulate concerning the nature of God this position is quite intelligible, but it cannot be taken as evidence for anything else but the existence of a particular view of the universe.

The case of the fig-tree brings out several important points which must be considered when dealing historically with the records of Jesus.

It shows the influence of a certain view of the supernatural upon the transmission of the record. Under this influence an event which in its original form appears a natural one is transformed into a preternatural one and so becomes part of the body of evidence for the "irruption" already spoken of. Hence it suggests that the same influence may have transformed many similar cases of natural into preternatural happenings. There is one case which Professor Hogg lays much stress on, the incident of the walking on the water. Careful comparison of the accounts in the Four Gospels makes a natural explanation of the episode perfectly tenable.

It is necessary then to remember that at a time when the modern conception of a realm of natural law did not exist in the popular mind at all, when all mental disease was regarded as demon-possession, when all phenomena whose causes were unknown or beyond human control were regarded as supernatural events, when dreams, hallucinations, and other vivid mental phenomena were objectified and regarded as Divine acts, when the ordinary events of life were invested with special moral significance, and a man born blind might be regarded as suffering the penalty of his parents' sins, when the movements of stars, comets, and other cosmic events were "intuitively apprehended" as having special appropriateness to individual situations—in such a time history was bound to be coloured by the general point of view, and

The Divine Intervention View 55

many occurrences would be so transformed in the telling as to become evidence for this irruption of cosmic energy into the realm of natural law.

It has been necessary to deal rather fully with this point because of its bearing on the evidence for the breaking in of redemptive energy.

When this principle of historical criticism is applied in detail to the "miraculous" events of the first century of Christianity in the same way in which we apply it without hesitation to mediaeval miracles or the stories of ancient secular history, a great shrinkage in the body of evidence for "preternatural" events takes place.

It may be remarked, in passing, that one of the preternatural events in the life of Jesus upon which great stress has been laid, his birth from a virgin, has no evidence of the slightest historical value. It is believed on religious and dogmatic grounds, not on historical grounds. The other great personal event, the resurrection, the historical evidence for which has already been discussed, will be dealt with later in relation to this view of Divine intervention.

First of all, it is necessary to say that here again the lack of proper historical evidence makes it very difficult to estimate correctly the significance of these acts of power. We find recorded in Mark the instantaneous healing of a case of fever, leprosy, flux, aphasia, a dead child (although Jesus is recorded as saying the child was not dead), two cases of blindness (one cure not instantaneous), two of paralysis, and four of demon-possession.

It is obviously not to be expected that exact details of these cases describing the symptoms and conditions under which the cure was effected, subsequent history of the cases, and so forth, could be given in an account written about half a century later by one who was not an eyewitness.

Yet such scientific exactitude is really necessary to establish the value of the cases as evidence for the breaking in of reserves of cosmic energy.

We have no means of knowing with any certainty whether we have before us cases of functional or organic disorder. It is obvious that in the last resort the balance will be swayed by a point of view based on other considerations than historical evidence.

But something still remains to be said on this point. It is clear from Mark's account, obscured as it is by lapse of time, and the inevitable effect of the general point of view of his age, as well as by the special point of view from which Jesus had come to be regarded by that time, that the exercise of Jesus' power depended on certain conditions. The οὐκ ἠδύνατο of Mark vi. 5, altered by Matthew in process of transmission, shows that Jesus was not always able to use his power. The accounts in Mark vii. 31-37 and viii. 22-26 of two cases in which external means were used, and in which the cure was not instantaneous, have been dropped by Matthew and Luke, as they suggest a view of the operation of Jesus' power which conflicted with the later conception of his unhindered wielding of omnipotence.

Hence, although Jesus may have believed that the power of God was at his disposal in a special way as the divinely-appointed instrument for the bringing in of the "new age," yet the documents seem to show that he discovered in actual practice that the use of this power depended on certain conditions. A very significant saying of his is recorded in Luke xii. 50 : " I have a baptism to be baptized with, and how am I straitened

The Divine Intervention View

till it be accomplished." It is impossible to tell in what precise situation the saying was originally uttered, but it vividly suggests his sense of baffled and thwarted desire. It certainly expresses his sense of that inadequate display of beneficent purpose in the realm of natural law of which Professor Hogg speaks. He felt that a world where lepers, blind, lame, paralytics, demoniacs, met the eye at every turn, where death prevailed, where men hated one another, where the rich oppressed the poor, and stronger nations dominated the weaker, was not a scene where the Father's "wealth of resource and benevolence of purpose" were adequately displayed. Moreover, whatever high hopes he may have felt at first as the result of his discovery of the power at his disposal, he came to realize how small and inadequate was the "irruption" resulting from his solitary efforts, and finally was led to stake everything upon his death as the means by which the real breach in the barrier might be achieved. What actually was achieved can only be estimated by the study of the early movement in Acts and later.

The question at present is whether the cures indicated by the gospel records afford us a basis for such an inference as Professor Hogg draws from them.

I cannot, in view of the scanty nature of the evidence, go beyond the suggestion that Jesus discovered the means of employing, through intense desire for the relief of suffering, passionate love for men, complete surrender of himself to what he believed to be God's purpose, certain powers which to-day are being discovered and used by psychiatrists, neuropathologists, and other specialists in mental disease.

The discovery and application by modern science of the laws governing the relations between mind and body, the direction of all this new knowledge to the relief of humanity is surely not evidence of the irruption of the supernatural but simply of the slow widening of the field of human knowledge to embrace and use natural forces hitherto beyond human control.

One more point must be touched on before we come to the question of the resurrection, that is, the belief that Jesus himself raised the dead. If he did the fact might certainly be sufficient to support Professor Hogg's argument for the irruption of the supernatural, whatever value the mere act of restoring people to the vicissitudes of life in a world like this might have.

There are three cases recorded—Jairus' daughter in the three Synoptic Gospels, the widow's son at Nain, only in Luke, and Lazarus, only in the Fourth Gospel.

In the reply of Jesus to the messengers of John, " the dead are raised " is given as part of the display of power offered as evidence to the messengers.

In the first case, the Marcan narrative, closely followed by the other two Synoptic Gospels, represents Jesus as saying that the child was not dead, for which he was ridiculed by those present. The parallel case of Eutychus in Acts xx. 7–12 may be noted. There the narrator clearly wishes to suggest that Paul restored the young man to life. At the same time he preserves Paul's words, " his life is in him."

It is not necessary to suppose then that the case of Jairus' daughter was more than a case of prolonged cataleptic state. Luke is the only source for the story of the widow's son. It is impossible to say anything of the value of Luke's source of information. The same explanation may hold good if the story is accepted as historical.

The case of Lazarus is different. It is as though the

The Divine Intervention View

author determined to remove all possibility of any suggestion that Lazarus was not really dead. He is dead four days before Jesus arrives, and the realism of the whole scene is familiar to all readers.

But the story raises the fundamental issue of the choice between the Synoptics and the Fourth Gospel as historical. The Fourth Gospel represents the incident as the climax of Jesus' life, the crowning miracle, witnessed by a large crowd of neutral spectators. The effect of it is such that the chief object of those who come to the Passover immediately following is to see the man who had been raised, and the miracle is represented by the author as the direct cause of the decision of the Sanhedrin to put Jesus to death without delay.

The Synoptists, whose ground-document is supposed to depend in a large measure upon the recollections of the most important eyewitness, Peter, have no mention of this crowning miracle, and are apparently ignorant of its bearing on the action of the authorities. For them the cleansing of the temple is the ultimate issue, the challenge to the priests' authority. Luke knows and mentions Martha and Mary but makes no mention of their brother. From what we know of his tendencies he is the last person to have omitted mention of such a notable evidence for the divine character of Jesus. It is also astonishing that the existence of such a witness to the Messiahship of Jesus is unmentioned in the story of the early movement in Jerusalem.

Since on other grounds we have good reason for believing that the author's purpose was not history but a mystical and allegorical representation of Jesus as the incarnation of the Divine reason, the living embodiment of light and life and joy in a dark and dying world, it is also reasonable, in view of the insuperable historical difficulties, to regard this story as the author's spiritual vision of Jesus as the Lord of life. Those whom he loves can never die.

Finally, with regard to the crucial example of this irruption of beneficent cosmic energy, the resurrection of Jesus himself, after examining the evidence it is difficult to avoid the conclusion that the evidence has been created by the belief, not the belief by the evidence. The real fact is that underlying the whole structure is a particular assumption or belief about God, which Professor Hogg so well sums up in the last extract quoted from his book. When once the development of this belief has been studied and traced from its earliest beginnings in pre-animistic religion many things become clear. The particular form of the religious belief of Jesus and his contemporaries about God takes its place in the historical development, and is explained by its relation to that development. I hope to deal with this question in another book. Here I have only tried to point out the historical difficulties which prevent me from accepting such a supernatural interpretation of the events of the life of Jesus and the early Church as Professor Hogg so attractively sets forth.

With one general consideration of a speculative nature I would close this over-long discussion.

A survey of the religious development of the human race shows that the roots of religion lie in the desire to establish relations with and to control the unknown forces with which man is surrounded. As those forces take on a personal form we find men's religious behaviour determined by the belief that the gods may be bound by spell, moved by prayer, appeased by sacrifice, induced to reward " righteous " conduct.

The Divine Intervention View

Throughout this period the underlying assumption is that the operation of the cosmic forces conceived as a personal mind and will may be favourably influenced on behalf of the individual.

In contrast with this attitude a new attitude which might well be called religious is arising to-day: it is the attitude of surrender to the facts of the universe. It is the attitude of patient and humble observation of the actual working of the universe, of spelling out letter by letter its mysterious runes, and of learning by such submission, such willingness to revise continually the results of knowledge, how to co-operate intelligently with the cosmic forces to what ever end they may be moving. Such an attitude involves for the present an acknowledgment of limitations, an agnosticism in the place of much that formerly seemed Divine certainty, but in the end it may prove to be the true way of life, the real surrender to the " Will of God."

APPENDIX

SYNOPTIC VIEW OF THE

Matthew xxvii. 57–61	*Mark xv. 42–47*
57. When it was late	42. When it was now late, because it was the preparation, i.e. the day before the sabbath,
there came a rich man from Arimathea by name Joseph	43. came Joseph from Arimathea.
	a councillor of good standing
who was himself a disciple of Jesus	who himself also was awaiting the Kingdom of God.
58. this man came to Pilate and claimed the body of Jesus	dared to go in to Pilate and claim the body of Jesus
	44. Pilate was amazed that he should be already dead and summoned a centurion and enquired of him if he had been dead some time
	45. and having learned this from the centurion
then Pilate ordered it to be given	he granted the corpse to Joseph
59. and Joseph took the body and wound it in clean linen	46. and having bought linen he took him down and wrapped him in the linen

Appendix

TO PART I

RESURRECTION NARRATIVES

Luke xxiii. 50–56	*John xix.* 38–42
	31. because it was the preparation.
	38. after these things
50. And behold a man by name Joseph [from Arimathea a city of the Jews] a councillor	Joseph of Arimathea
51. a good and just man who had not been a party to their plan and its execution who was awaiting the Kingdom of God.	
52. this man went in to Pilate and claimed the body of Jesus	a disciple of Jesus but secretly for fear of the Jews asked Pilate that he might take away the body of Jesus.
	and Pilate consented.
53. and having taken it down he wound it in linen	So he came and took away his body

Matthew	Mark
60. and laid it in his own new grave which he had cut in the rock	and laid him in a tomb which was cut out of the rock
and rolled a great stone to the door of the grave and departed	and rolled a stone to the door of the grave
61. And there were there Mary Magdalene and the other Mary sitting opposite the burial place	47. And Mary Magdalene and Mary (the mother) of Joses were watching where he was laid
[62–66] [The setting of the watch at the grave (only in Matthew.)]	
xxviii. 1–10	*xvi.* 1–8
1. but late on the sabbath	1. And when the sabbath was past

Appendix

Luke   *John*

                   39. And Nicodemus also came, who came to him by night at the first, bringing a mixture of myrrh and aloes, about a hundred pounds weight.

                   40. So he took the body of Jesus, and bound it with grave clothes with the spices, as is the custom of the Jews to bury.

and placed him in a tomb of hewn stone   41. Now in the place where he was crucified was an orchard and in the orchard a new grave where no one had yet been laid. So there, because of the Jews' preparation, since the grave was near, they laid Jesus.

where no one had yet lain

55. and some women following after, who had come with him out of Galilee, watched the grave and how his body was laid and went back and prepared spices and perfumes.
Now on the sabbath they kept quiet according to the law,

     xxiv. 1–12   *xx*

                                1. on the first day of the week

Matthew	Mark
came Mary Magdalene and the other Mary	Mary Magdalene and Mary (the mother) of James and Salome bought spices
to see the burial place	that they might come and anoint him.
	2. and very early
[as it was growing dusk towards the first day of the week]	on the first day of the week they come to the tomb at sunrise
2. and behold there was a great earthquake, for an angel of the Lord descended from heaven and came and rolled away the stone and sat on it	
3. and his face was like lightning and his clothing white as snow. For fear of him those who were guarding the grave shook and became as dead.	
	3. and they were saying to one another who will roll away for us the stone from the door of the grave
	4. and looking up they see that the stone has been rolled away for it was very great
	5. and entering into the grave

Appendix

Luke *John*

Mary Magdalene

1. but on the first day of the week
   very early
   they came to the tomb
   bringing the spices which they had prepared.

   comes

   early while it is still dark
   to the grave

2. and they found
   the stone
   rolled away from the grave

   and sees the stone
   taken away from the grave

3. and entering in

Matthew *Mark*

	they saw a young man
	sitting to the right
	clothed in a white garment
	and they were much alarmed

5. and the angel answered and said to the women,
be not afraid
for I know that you are seeking
the crucified Jesus.
6. he is not here for
he is risen,
as he said;
come, see the place
where he lay
7. and go quickly
say to his disciples
that he is risen from the dead and behold he goes before you into Galilee
there shall ye see him;
behold, I have told you.

6. and he said to them

do not be alarmed.
You are seeking Jesus,

the crucified Nazarene,
he is risen,
he is not here;

see the place
where they laid him
7. but go away
and say to his disciples
and to Peter
that he goes before you
into Galilee
there shall ye see him,
as he told you.

8. And going away quickly   8. And coming out they fled

Appendix

Luke   *John*

they did not find the body of the Lord Jesus	
4. and while they were perplexed about this behold two men stood by them in shining apparel,	12. she sees two angels in white sitting, one at the head and one at the feet where the body of Jesus had lain
5. and as they were afraid and bowed down their faces to the ground, they said to them	and they say to her woman, why weepest thou?
why do you seek the living among the dead,	
6. he is not here, but is risen ;	
remember how he said to you	
while he was still in Galilee	
7. saying the Son of Man must be delivered into the hands of sinners and crucified and the third day rise again	
8. And they remembered his words	
9. And returning	

Matthew	Mark
from the grave with fear and great joy they ran to bring the news to his disciples	from the grave for trembling and panic seized them
	and they said nothing to anyone for they were afraid of . . .
9. And behold Jesus met them, saying, Greeting. And they came and held him by the feet and worshipped him. 10. Then Jesus said to them, Fear not, go tell my brethren to go away to Galilee and there they will see me.	[Here the original ending of Mark breaks off with an unfinished sentence]

Appendix

Luke   *John*

from the grave

they announced all these things to the eleven and to all the rest.

10. It was Mary Magdalene and Joanna and Mary (the mother) of James and the rest with them who told these things to
11. the apostles, and these things seemed nonsense to them and they disbelieved them.

PART II

THE RISE OF THE MOVEMENT IN JERUSALEM

CHAPTER I

THE MEANING OF PENTECOST

AT the beginning of one of the later of the early Christian documents, the letter to the Hebrews, there occurs a passage which well illustrates the general point of view from which the first stage of the Christian movement was regarded at the close of the first century: " How shall we escape if we neglect so great salvation, which at the first began to be spoken by the Lord, and was confirmed unto us by them that heard Him, God also bearing them witness by signs and miracles and divers powers and gifts of the Holy Ghost according to His own will " (Heb. ii. 3, 4).

We are able now to begin the task of examining the historical grounds upon which this point of view rests.

For the earliest stage of all, the beginnings of the movement in Jerusalem, we have no evidence but the opening chapters of Acts. The main historical value of Paul's letters belongs to the second stage.

It is generally recognized that Luke and Acts form two parts of a single historical work. We know that in the first part of the work the author has made use of at least one documentary source, Mark, and we can follow his methods in the use of such a source. We have no direct evidence for a similar use of documentary sources in his second book, but a careful examination of the narrative suggests that the second book like the first is a product of the skilful use of various sources. For a full discussion of the problem of the sources of Acts the student may be referred to Harnack's "Acts of the Apostles," and especially to Chapter V of Volume II of Jackson and Lake's "The Beginnings of Christianity."

If we read through the first five chapters of Acts the narrative appears to present a continuous story relating the intercourse of Jesus with his disciples in Jerusalem during the forty days between his resurrection and ascension, the ten days of waiting in the upper room between the Ascension and Pentecost, the choice of an apostle to fill the place of Judas, the account of Pentecost, the first preaching, the mode and life of the first community in Jerusalem, the healing of the lame man and its results, and the story of Ananias and Sapphira.

Now, first of all, we have to consider the problem created by the discovery that the resurrection narratives prove the existence of two distinct and historically incompatible traditions, the Jerusalem tradition and the Galilean tradition. We have seen that the author of Luke–Acts accepts the Jerusalem tradition and so modifies his most important source as to remove the traces of this tradition. Hence it must be supposed that the same process would have to be continued in the second book. Anything suggesting the return of the disciples from Galilee to Jerusalem would disappear in the editing of the sources.

Now we are proceeding on the assumption that the balance of historical probability lies with the Galilean tradition, hence the account in Acts i., which continues the Jerusalem tradition of Luke xxiv. and leaves no

The Meaning of Pentecost

place for the flight of the disciples to Galilee, their experiences there, and subsequent return to Jerusalem, falls into the same category as the events of Luke xxiv.

Secondly, careful examination of the first five chapters of Acts shows the existence of a number of doublets, a literary phenomenon which in the criticism of the Pentateuch and of the Synoptic Gospels, as in many other instances, has served to indicate the presence of parallel sources. The student can compare these doublets and form his own conclusions as to the results which they appear to suggest. In tabular form they appear as follows:

The Gift of the Spirit:
        Acts ii. 1-13.   Acts iv. 31.
The Preaching of Peter:
        Acts ii. 14-36.   Acts iii. 12-26.
The Resultant Conversion:
        Acts ii. 37-41.   Acts iv. 4.
Communism:
        Acts ii. 42-47.   Acts iv 34-37.
Arrest and Trial of Apostles:
        Acts v. 17-41.   Acts iv. 1-3, 5-22.

In the first of these doublets a wide divergence is observable between the two accounts. In the first account the most striking detail, and one which is said to have attracted widespread attention, is the phenomenon of glossolalia, or speaking with tongues. In the second account, while the same group is again said to be filled with the Spirit, no mention of tongues occurs.

Now in this particular case we are able to check the account of glossolalia given in Acts ii. 1-13 by the account of a first-hand witness, Paul himself, who not only had experienced " tongues," but gives a full and interesting account of the existence and nature of this abnormal psychological phenomenon as he had observed it in a primitive Christian community, viz. at Corinth. The student can compare Paul's account in 1 Corinthians xiv. with the account given in Acts ii. 1–13. From Paul's account it is evident that the person who spoke a tongue neither understood himself what was uttered nor was he understood by those who heard him. A further gift, that of interpretation, was needed to make the gift of glossolalia of any value to the ecclesia. Paul evidently attaches small importance to glossolalia.

Paul's account is so obviously in contradiction with the account in Acts ii. 1–13 as to suggest the unhistorical character of the source which the author of Acts is using.

Without working out the comparison of the doublets in detail, the result is to suggest the existence of two parallel sources which the author has worked up into a continuous narrative.

The first source is probably the continuation of the Jerusalem source for Luke xxiv. It comprises Acts i.–ii. and v.17–41. The second source comprises Acts iii.–iv.35. It is uncertain whether Acts iv. 36–v. 16 belongs to the first or the second source. Now a comparison of the two sources raises several interesting questions.

In the first place, if Acts iii.–iv. 35 be regarded as a parallel source for the history of the first events in Jerusalem, it suggests that it must have originally contained an account of the events which lie between Mark xvi. 1–8 and the unexplained presence of Peter and John in the temple at Jerusalem.

That is, just as the end of the resurrection story, which almost certainly would have given us the experience of the disciples in Galilee, has been cut off

The Meaning of Pentecost

to make room for the Jerusalem tradition as it appears in Luke xxiv., so the beginning of the source contained in Acts iii.-iv. 35, which would have explained how the disciples returned from Galilee to Jerusalem, has been cut off and skilfully fitted by the author of Luke-Acts into the Jerusalem tradition.

Harnack, who has based his analysis of sources rather upon the locality from which traditions might have proceeded than upon persons round whom they might have grown up, has called these two sources Jerusalem-B and Jerusalem-A respectively, and regards the Jerusalem-A source, Acts iii.-iv. 35, as the earlier and more historical of the two.

Some of the results of the comparison of the two sources will be dealt with later.

Meanwhile let us attempt to continue, on the basis of this analysis, the reconstruction of the Galilean tradition begun in Chapter X of the first section of this book.

It was suggested there that as the result of their experiences in Galilee the disciples decided to come back to Jerusalem. In all probability they had no definite plan, and on their arrival waited for some sign of the fulfilment of those expectations which Jesus had kindled in their minds.

During this time of waiting the point at which Luke joins our source to his Jerusalem tradition represents Peter and John (whether John the son of Zebedee or John Mark we cannot tell) as going to the Temple to pray.

A lame beggar attracts Peter's attention. The thought comes to Peter that it may be that the power which he had often seen working when Jesus was with them, a power which, according to the Gospel narrative, Jesus had to some extent imparted to the disciples, is still operative.

With a great leap of faith he commands the lame man to walk. The effect electrifies both Peter and the bystanders. However we may explain it now, the act was immediately interpreted as an act of Divine intervention.

Public attention was roused, the authorities inquired into the matter and were unable to cast any doubt on the genuineness of the cure. Peter's explanation of what had happened was extremely distasteful to them and showed dangerous tendencies. However, it was impossible to punish such an act, so the authorities dismissed Peter and his companion with a warning. Peter and John returned to the rest of the group and told them what had happened. The result was that the whole group, inspired by the same confidence and faith, "filled with the Holy Spirit," began to preach boldly in Jerusalem. No mention is made of "tongues."

Such would seem to be the earlier, simpler story of an undated occurrence which in a later tradition was assigned to the date of the Jewish feast of Weeks and was retold with the amplification which marks the account of Pentecost in Acts ii. 1–13. It may well be that this experience represents the basis of the story of the appearance to the eleven which Luke relates in the Gospel as having taken place in Jerusalem.

How rapidly the movement spread it is impossible to say. One source represents three thousand as joining the movement in one day, the other speaks of five thousand. The Oriental tendency to exaggerate numbers is a commonplace of history. But undoubtedly the movement found the soil prepared and was not slow in developing. We have next to inquire what were the beliefs and outlook of this primitive community in Jerusalem.

CHAPTER II

CHARACTERISTICS OF THE PRIMITIVE COMMUNITY

WE are so accustomed to think and speak of the primitive community in Jerusalem as the Christian Church that it is somewhat of a shock to discover from a study of the early records that there is not a single distinctively Christian feature in the belief, outlook, and organization of that community.

How far the speeches in Acts represent actual reports of the words of the speakers in the situations related is a difficult problem. It is well known that the current practice of historians was to put into the mouths of their personages speeches that seemed to them fitting for the occasion described. Shorthand reporters did not attend meetings in those days. The accounts of these early days were not written down until many years after. Nevertheless, the very absence from these records of the early preaching of those elements of belief which so soon became characteristic of Christianity suggests that they represent more or less faithfully the point of view of the primitive community. Hence we may use them as a basis for the reconstruction of the belief of the earliest community.

If we take the speech of Peter in Acts iii. as representing the earliest tradition of the outlook of the movement and its leaders, we find the following significant facts:

Jesus is described as the *Servant* of the God of the

Jews. He is the holy righteous man who has been rejected by the Jews and their rulers in ignorance of his true character. He is described as the Leader of life (ἀρχηγὸν τῆς ζωῆς). He has been raised from the dead, a fact of which the speakers claim to be witnesses, though no details are given. He is the Messiah whom God has predestined for the Jews (τὸν προκεχειρισμένον ὑμῖν χριστόν), his death is the fulfilment of prophecy. He is now in heaven waiting for the establishment of the new age. If the Jews repent, their guilt in rejecting him will be annulled and he will at once return to set up the kingdom and fulfil the promises made to the fathers. He is the Prophet whose coming Moses foretold.

In this report no mention is made of the gift of the Spirit or of baptism.

The Messiahship of Jesus and his return to set up the kingdom are the fundamental ideas here. The acceptance of these ideas involved absolutely no break with any characteristic Jewish beliefs except such as might be involved in the possibility of the death of the Messiah.

The description of the life of the community which follows the report of this address gives us a picture of what is commonly spoken of as "the communistic experiment" of the primitive community. The motive, however, as Paul's letters bear witness (cf. 1 Cor. vii. 29-31) was not a revolt from the social conditions of the day but the consequence of the apocalyptic outlook. The daily expectation of the return of the Messiah destroyed the usually operative motives underlying the possession of property.

The state of this same community several years later at the time of Paul's arrest in Jerusalem is described in Acts xxi. 20. It is true that certain important developments had taken place in the meantime which

Characteristics of Primitive Community 81

will be dealt with in due course, but the picture in Acts xxi. 20 of a numerous body under the leadership of James the Lord's brother, living peacefully in Jerusalem, observing the Mosaic law and the usual practices of Jewish religious life, shows the real character of this primitive community whose beginning is here described. The parallel account of the early preaching as given in Acts ii. 14–36 adds some details to the general picture of the belief and practice of the primitive community. Some of these details probably represent a slightly later stage of development, but still belong to the beginnings of the movement.

First of all, we find the beginnings of a doctrine of the Spirit. Again it is necessary to put ourselves back into an attitude which is wholly different from the Christian view.

Two connected lines of thought had grown up in Jewish circles. All manifestations of the prophetic gift were thought to be the result of the presence of the spirit of God in the person gifted; and further, a special outpouring of the spirit upon the regenerated Israel was announced by the later prophets as a sign of the last days.

Jesus regarded himself as doing his works of power by the spirit of God. He promised the disciples that when the time came for them to make their defence before the authorities the spirit of their Father would speak in them. He was regarded by the early community as specially anointed by God with the spirit (Acts x. 38).

In this address he is regarded as elevated to the Messiahship through resurrection, and as having received a special gift of the spirit. He has poured out this gift of the spirit as a fulfilment of the prophecy in Joel ii. and as a sign that the last days have begun.

Secondly, in dealing with the resurrection we find no appeal to the empty grave or to first-hand testimony of appearances to eyewitnesses, but an appeal to the fulfilment of Old Testament Scriptures, the beginning of a line of argument which develops during the first two centuries until the whole of the Old Testament comes to be regarded as a storehouse of prophetic testimonies to the coming of Jesus.

Thirdly, we have the introduction of the rite of baptism as the means of marking out the new community, the sect of the Nazarenes as they were at first called, from their Jewish compatriots.

Hence the picture that we get is one of a Jewish sect or community, holding fast to the main beliefs of Judaism, loyal to the temple, but believing that the historical Jesus of Nazareth was the Messiah of prophecy, and expecting his immediate return to establish the new age. This belief constituted them a separate body, a sect, such as the Essenes and other communities already formed. Their inner life was marked by enthusiasm, by the spring and power of their hope in the speedy return of Jesus.

This was the " great salvation " for which they looked, a deliverance from the present evil age, and a triumphant introduction into the new world order, where Jesus would be manifested as Messiah and Divine Ruler and Judge, and their faith in him finally vindicated.

It is a far cry from such a picture to Nicæa and Augustine's City of God, and our problem now is to reconstruct as far as it is possible the main stages of development which changed the obscure " sect of the Nazarenes " into the heir of the Imperial power of the Cæsars.

CHAPTER III

THE FIRST CRISIS AND ITS CAUSES

BEFORE we go on to discuss the causes of the first crisis in the history of the primitive community there are certain general considerations about the " tendency " of Acts that need to be dealt with.

We have a first-hand witness to the inner side of the history of the break with Judaism—the letters of Paul. A comparison of his letters with the story told by the author or redactor of Acts makes it clear that certain fundamental features of the story have been smoothed over or so far obliterated as to give us a distorted picture of the early stages of the movement. Not only does a comparison of the first two chapters of Galatians, with the parallel story in Acts, make it clear that serious historical discrepancies exist, but the whole tenor of Galatians and Corinthians shows that a much sharper and bitterer cleavage existed between the parties in the early Church than we should gather from the story in Acts.

Moreover, just as we have seen that Acts is silent concerning the Galilean tradition and its place in the founding of the movement, so there is evidence of the gaps in the history of the movement. The story of Paul's conversion indicates the presence of a Christian community in Damascus whose origin and growth is unexplained.

We have hints of the growth of a movement connected with John the Baptist that had spread as far as Ephesus and possibly Alexandria and whose relations to the Christian movement are reflected in the Fourth Gospel.

A Christian community had been founded in Rome that did not owe its origin to Paul.

Hence it is clear that many important factors in the whole development have been omitted by the redactor of Acts in the interests of his theory of the growth of the Church and its relations with the mother-church, as he regards it, at Jerusalem, with the Jews, and with the Imperial authorities.

It is necessary to bear these considerations in mind as we go on to reconstruct the history with the help of Paul's letters.

Underlying the story of the appointment of the seven deacons and the martyrdom of Stephen and its consequences we find the elements which brought about the first fundamental disruption of the primitive community. We find mentioned for the first time and without explanation the existence of two parties in the primitive community at Jerusalem—the Hebrews and the Hellenists. It is well known that " Hebrews " is the technical term for Aramaic-speaking Jews of Palestinian birth, while " Hellenists " signifies Greek-speaking Jews of the Dispersion living in Jerusalem, or Gentile proselytes who had been circumcized and so become members of the Jewish community. While it was possible for Hellenists to be strict Jews, yet in general the difference in speech and social customs involved a more liberal attitude towards religion. The Hellenistic Jews appear to have had various synagogues of their own in Jerusalem.

Underlying the story of the appointment of the seven

The First Crisis and its Causes

deacons by the Twelve Apostles and the rather obscure details of the trivial dispute which gave rise to their appointment is the fundamental fact of the separate organization of the two sections in Jerusalem.

The seven have all Greek names, and one of them is a proselyte from Antioch.

It seems fairly evident that the redactor is here putting back into the primitive period the origin of the later organization of the Christian Churches. It is worth observing that although the previous chapters describe the apostles as concerned with the financial administration of the little community, yet here they are represented as repudiating this function and as assuming the functions of preaching and liturgical administration later characteristic of the bishops. Moreover, the seven, although appointed to financial administration (if that is the meaning of " serving tables "), are subsequently represented as wholly engaged in preaching, and we hear nothing of their administrative work.

The fact is that here, as elsewhere, the redactor has partially obscured the real state of affairs in his effort to depict what he conceived to be the history of the development. As elsewhere he smoothes over the sharp cleavage between the Gentile church and the Judaisers so here he obscures the origin of this cleavage.

Nevertheless, the nature of the crisis emerges. We have a clear picture of the first definite conflict with the priestly authorities at Jerusalem. While it is very doubtful whether Stephen's speech is genuine, and its contents bear only a slight relation to the actual situation, yet the real issue is well summed up in the accusation which is laid against Stephen before the

Sanhedrin: "We have heard him say that Jesus the Nazarene shall destroy this place and change the customs which Moses delivered to us."

The Hellenists had found in the spirit of the Nazarene an energy which was destined to break through the narrow bounds of Judaism.

A relentless persecution against the Hellenists broke out. It began with the execution or lynching of Stephen and led to the complete dispersion of the Hellenist adherents of the Nazarene sect at Jerusalem.

An apparently casual reference to the apostles, a phrase that usually passes unnoticed, shows to what an extent the real nature of the crisis has been obliterated by the redactor. In Acts viii. 1 we are told that the whole church in Jerusalem was scattered, "*except the apostles.*" The heads of the movement are left untouched, and, if we take the redactor's account, are left without a community to guide. But almost immediately after, the account of Paul's conversion, as well as the controversy raised by the admission of the Gentile Cornelius to the community, shows that an important body of Jewish Christians, as we may call them by anticipation, still remained in Jerusalem. The real facts of the case, obscured by the redactor's unhistorical account, are that the first great cleavage destined to affect the whole subsequent development of the movement had taken place.

The liberal Hellenist party was driven from Jerusalem and forced to disperse. Antioch in Syria became their new centre. The Hebraists, with the apostles at their head, remained comparatively unmolested in Jerusalem. A growing divergence appears between the Jerusalem community under the leadership of

The First Crisis and its Causes

James the Lord's brother, and the communities which arose as a result of the activities of the dispersed Hellenists.

The community in Jerusalem remained faithful to the temple, the law, and the ancestral customs of the race. The Hellenists, whose general position may be represented by Paul's letters, stood for an increasing measure of freedom from the law.

The result was a period of strife and bitterness between the two parties, a struggle which Paul never ceased to wage till the day of his death. The outcome of the struggle is strange and unexpected.

Before passing on to our next section, which deals with the work of Paul and the growth of the Hellenist movement, we may pause to sum up results.

Jesus had seen a vision of a new order and a new spirit working amongst men. He had imparted something of his vision to his small band of followers before his death. The shock of that disaster drove the little party of Galileans back to their homes.

But the impression made by Jesus upon those who had lived with him during the short but crowded time of his career was too deep to be eradicated.

Faith and hope returned in Galilee. The spirit of Jesus lived on in his followers. The primitive tradition singles out Peter as the first to whom came the conviction that Jesus was still alive.

Under his leadership the band returned to Jerusalem to seek opportunity to carry out the vision of Jesus. Their faith was confirmed by the evidence of the power of the name of Jesus in the healing of the lame man, and they began to announce publicly in Jerusalem the resurrection of Jesus, his Messiahship and immediate return. A community or sect was formed whose general characteristics have already been described in the previous chapter.

Then the spread of their beliefs to the Hellenistic circle in Jerusalem introduced a new element and led to the formation of another party having its own leaders. This liberal wing quickly attracted the attention of the Jewish authorities and was driven from Jerusalem by persecution, while the older body of Hebraist adherents were left to grow in Jerusalem under the ultimate leadership of James.

We have a picture of Peter wavering between the two positions and finally disappearing.

The author or redactor of Acts, probably in the interest of the Roman tradition, seeks to represent Peter and Paul as equal in dignity, to obliterate their conflict, and to depict Peter as the originator of the Gentile mission, but the historicity of this picture is extremely doubtful.

PART III

PAUL AND THE TRANSITION

CHAPTER I

PAUL IN ACTS

THE main historical problem in this stage of our inquiry is the one created by a comparison of Paul's summary in Gal. i.–ii. of the first fourteen years of his Christian career with the account given by the redactor of Acts of the same period.

In his letter to the Galatians, Paul has a very definite object in view. The Galatian churches have been visited by a Judaizing mission, apparently with the authority of the mother-church at Jerusalem behind them. Their object is to show the Galatians that Paul has omitted vital religious necessities in his instruction. It is necessary to be circumcized and to keep the law of Moses in certain respects.

Paul's object is to prove to the Galatians that his message is original and independent of the Judaizing leaders at Jerusalem. He gives a brief sketch of his life from his conversion up to the moment of writing in order to prove the extent of his intercourse with the Jerusalem community. He guarantees the truth of his account by a solemn asseveration.

Before examining the problem it may be useful to set out in parallel columns the accounts given by Paul and the redactor of Acts.

Christianity in the Making

Galatians	Acts
i. 15 Conversion	ix. 1–18 Conversion at Damascus (Cf. 2 Cor. xi. 32, 33)
i. 17 Did not go to Jerusalem, went into Arabia, returned to Damascus	
i. 18 After *three years* went to Jerusalem, stayed 15 days, saw only Peter and James	ix. 23 After *many days* (ἡμέραι ἱκαναί) driven out, came to Jerusalem, was introduced to apostles by Barnabas
	ix. 30 driven out, went to Tarsus
i. 21 Returned to Syria and Cilicia	ix. 32–x. 48 Peter's activity in south-west Judæa and Cæsarea. Conversion of Cornelius
	xi. 1–18 Acceptance of Peter's action by Jerusalem Church
	xi. 19–24 Founding of church in Syria, Antioch, by dispersed Hellenists
	xi. 25–25 Barnabas brings Paul from Tarsus to Antioch. He stays *one year*
ii. 1 After *fourteen years* went to Jerusalem with Barnabas and Titus, "by revelation"	xi. 30 Paul goes to Jerusalem with Barnabas bringing famine relief

Paul in Acts

Galatians	*Acts*
ii. 2 Private interview with heads of Jerusalem Church	xii. 1-19 Herod's persecution. Martyrdom of James, the son of Zebedee (and probably John). Peter imprisoned; escapes and goes to Cæsarea
ii. 7-10 Leaders approve Paul's mission to Gentiles, urge need of poor	xii. 25 Paul and Barnabas return to Antioch
ii. 11 Peter comes to Antioch	xiii. 4-xiv. 28 Paul and Barnabas make first journey through South Galatia; return to Antioch and spent a long time (χρόνον οὐκ ὀλίγον) there
	xv. 1 Judaizing mission from Jerusalem comes to Antioch
ii. 12 Mission from James to Antioch, defection of Peter and Barnabas	xv. 3 Paul and Barnabas sent to Jerusalem
	xv. 6-29 Apostolic Council and Decrees
	xv. 36 Second journey begins
	xvi. 4 Decrees of Apostolic Council delivered to South Galatian churches.

Perhaps the first and most striking contrast, not necessarily involving any discrepancy, is the definite note of time in Paul's account as compared with the parallel story in Acts. Paul is explicit that a period of fourteen years intervenes between his conversion and the episode at Jerusalem, which seems to correspond with the account of the Apostolic Council in Acts xv. It would be difficult to infer so long a period of time from Acts, but comparison shows that no necessary discrepancy is involved. The "many days" of Acts ix. 23 agrees with Paul's three years in Damascus, Gal. i. 18; and the "long time" of Acts xiv. 28 at Antioch will account for the remaining eleven years which make up Paul's fourteen years from his conversion.

The real contrast lies in the comparative silence of Acts as to the events outside Jerusalem which have occupied those fourteen years.

We perceive that during these years an immense activity was at work, which, starting from the dispersion of the Hellenists after Stephen's death, had resulted in the establishment of a movement with its centre at Syrian Antioch definitely embracing Gentiles as well as Hellenistic Jews.

Of the profound differences between the Jerusalem community and the new movement we should gather little from Acts. It is only where we read Paul's letters that we see how deep and far-reaching Paul conceived the divergence to be. In Paul the antithesis between "Christian" and "Jew" first becomes distinct, and one understands that, in the casual statement, "the disciples were first called Christians at Antioch," there is far more than meets the eye.

From Acts we should gather that every stage of the

forward movement was either initiated or sanctioned by Jerusalem, that there were no sharp contrasts or lines of cleavage, and that Paul from the first had the approval of the apostles at Jerusalem.

From Galatians we receive the picture of an independent development only coming into official contact with Jerusalem fourteen years after its beginning. Paul's letters are the only source we have whence we can draw some idea of the beliefs and practices of this movement, and in the next chapter we shall attempt an outline of this new position.

The main point here is the realization that we have not to do with a single type of " Christianity," distinguished from the outset by its doctrines and practices from Judaism, but with a movement which developed successively a number of different forms according to the environment and historical conditions under which it arose.

The solution of the particular problem which the above comparison of Acts and Galatians raises is not of much importance compared with the recognition of what the difference between the two accounts involves.

The Paul of Acts is approved at the outset by the apostles, brings famine relief from Antioch to Jerusalem, and receives official instructions from the heads of the Jerusalem community which he faithfully delivers to the Hellenistic communities which he had founded. The Paul of the letters passionately affirms the independent authority of his mission as directly received from " the Lord," denies all relations with the Jerusalem authorities during the fourteen years of expansion, save a brief fortnight's visit to Jerusalem, in which he saw only Peter and James. He writes and acts in apparent entire ignorance that any authoritative instructions had been issued from Jerusalem which could affect the Galatians, the Corinthians, or the Romans.

He regards the attitude of Jerusalem as "Judaizing," as a return to "bondage," as the complete frustration of all that the spirit of Christ involved for him.

It is not the plan of this book to deal with the historical problems of Acts in detail, but to sketch out broadly the successive phases through which the Christian movement passed until its beliefs and practices and organization became fixed in creed, sacramental system, and official hierarchy.

Hence it is sufficient for this purpose to indicate the tendency of Acts and the main stages of the movement which it covers.

These stages are, first, the founding of a Jewish Messianic community in Jerusalem, then the growth of a Hellenistic community within the primitive group, the divergence of this Hellenistic body from the parent community, its persecution by the Jewish religious authorities, its scattering and the beginning of a Gentile mission with headquarters at Antioch. Then Paul's conversion, adherence to the Hellenistic community, and through his amazing labours the spread of the new movement through Asia Minor to Greece and Rome.

The redactor of Acts has so far succeeded in minimizing the differences between the primitive body and the new movement as to represent a continuous development of an anti-Jewish religion, usually favoured by the Roman provincial authorities, and always persecuted by local Jewish animosity. He proves that Christians are not Jews, and that the protagonist of the movement is a Roman citizen, always respectful of imperial authority; he leaves his hero settled in the imperial city peacefully teaching under Roman protection and disowning all Jewish affiliations. But of the inner spirit of the movement we learn little from Acts.

For that we must turn to Paul's letters.

CHAPTER II

PAUL AND THE PRIMITIVE TRADITION

WE have seen that in Acts the general character of the Hellenistic or Antiochene movement, where the name Christian first came into being, is suggested by the summing up of the charge against Stephen. Looked at broadly, it was a break from Jewish law and custom. But from Acts we learn little or nothing of the depth of religious experience and the breadth of external religious environment involved in this movement.

It will always be a difficult, perhaps insoluble, problem to determine how great a degree of divergence or similarity lies between Jerusalem and Antioch. For instance, we have the position suggested by Professor E. F. Scott in his admirable little book "The Beginnings of the Church" (Scribners, 1914). He insists on Paul's dependence on the primitive church: "New Testament criticism is now retreating from this position, so long accepted as self-evident, that the work of Paul was altogether revolutionary. It is coming to be recognized, in view of a more exact study of his life and writings, that he owed far more to the primitive church than has usually been granted, and that his relation to it was one of substantial sympathy."

Further, Professor Scott emphasizes the continuity between the message of Jesus and the primitive church: "The message of Jesus had worked itself into the life

Paul and the Primitive Tradition

of the church and so passed down to the next generation as its most precious heritage." Again : " The teaching of Jesus was a living power in the church and all its beliefs and activities were influenced directly by that teaching."

On the other hand, we have the position which Professor Scott is opposing, a very widely held one, that a profound and fundamental divergence existed between Paul's teaching and the type represented by the Jerusalem church, and further, that neither of these two divergent tendencies is the heir of the teaching of Jesus.

The issues thus raised can only be referred back to the documents themselves. The contrast between the preaching reported in the early chapters of Acts and the teaching of Jesus is obvious. The early preaching is a message of the death, resurrection, Messiahship, and advent of Jesus. Nevertheless it is possible to say with entire probability, as Harnack does, that alongside of this preaching " the words of Jesus of course exercised a silent and effective mission of their own, whilst the historical picture furnished by the gospels, together with faith in the exalted Christ, exerted a powerful influence over catechumens and believers " (" Mission and Expansion of Christianity," Vol. I, p. 42).

With regard to the agreement between the Jewish and Hellenistic positions the unemphasized situation suggested by the casual notice in Acts viii. 1 points to a more fundamental difference than the redactor of Acts would admit. The Jerusalem authorities who drive out the Hellenist section allow the apostles and the Hebraist section to remain unmolested in Jerusalem.

The extent of Paul's own agreement with or divergence from the primitive tradition can only be determined by reference to his own letters. Even here, however, in dealing with his own account of his attitude there are certain reservations to be made.

First, Paul is concerned in some of the letters which contain the frankest statements of his own experience to assert as strongly as possible his independence of tradition. Hence we may expect a minimizing of his debt to the common tradition.

Secondly, since the letters deal more with controverted points and new developments, the broad outline of his preaching, those matters in which a large measure of agreement with tradition might be expected, are not elaborated. Hence, again, difference rather than agreement tends to be emphasized.

Lastly, it must be remembered that Paul cannot be taken as entirely typical of Hellenistic Christianity. His experience was so individual, and his working out of the implications of that experience so peculiarly his own, that his influence on the subsequent course of church doctrine is far less than is commonly supposed. The Paul of Augustinian and Lutheran theology is as far removed from the real Paul as the Aristotle of Aquinas is from the real Aristotle.

CHAPTER III

STATEMENT OF THE PROBLEMS

PAUL was not the only torch-bearer of the Gentile mission. His earliest associate, Barnabas, was possibly the founder of the Christian community at Antioch, and there were many nameless refugees who fled from Jerusalem and spread the new teaching in the Roman Empire.

But Paul was the outstanding figure of the Gentile mission for the first twenty years of its history, and the Church has accepted his own designation of himself as "the Apostle of the Gentiles." His letters are almost our only first-hand evidence for the beliefs and practices of the early Christian communities outside Palestine during the first stage of their growth.

It would be impossible within the limits of the space at our disposal to attempt a full description and discussion of Paul's experience and of the system which he built up out of his experience. We must limit our discussion to the following main points:

(i) The nature of the "tradition" which Paul received from the primitive community and handed on to his converts in Asia Minor and Greece.

(ii) The essential differences between Paul's teaching and the position of the Hebraist community at Jerusalem as far as we know it from Acts and from Paul's references to the points at issue.

(iii) The nature of the background and environment to which the message that Paul brought was obliged to adapt itself in language and forms of thought.
(iv) The way in which Paul was obliged to think out the place of Jesus and his significance in the new movement.

CHAPTER IV

PAUL AND THE SPIRIT

IN the fifteenth chapter of Paul's first letter to the Corinthians he gives a summary of the "tradition" which he had received and handed on to the community at Corinth. It consists only of the death, burial, and resurrection of Christ, "according to the Scriptures," and of the appearances of the risen Christ as fixed by the tradition. The institution of the Lord's supper (1 Cor. xi. 23), the belief in the Parousia (1 Thess. iv. 15), are also elements in the "tradition" which Paul had received.

The general outline of the future coming of the kingdom as described in 1 Cor. xv., and elsewhere, is probably part of the common eschatological tradition (cf. 1 Thess. v. 1).

We can also infer that Paul's knowledge of the character of Jesus and the few indirect references to his teaching were derived from the primitive tradition.

It is possible that the collection of proof-texts from the Old Testament, which took very early the form of a Testimony Book for use in controversy with the Jews, had its origin in Jerusalem. Professor Rendel Harris has shown conclusively that Paul knew and used this primitive collection of Testimonies.

The Messiahship of Jesus, the belief in his near return to establish the Kingdom of God and to judge the world, the fulfilment of the Old Testament prophecies in the life and death of Jesus, and the sovereignty of God are the main elements which Paul received from the primitive Jerusalem tradition.

We know from Acts that along with this simple body of primitive belief the early community at Jerusalem also retained their belief in the validity of the Jewish law and adherence to the worship of the temple.

It was here that the main divergence between Hebraist and Hellenist arose. Already among the Jews of the Dispersion the claims of the ritual law and of the minutiæ of Jewish religious custom had been considerably weakened.

But Paul's own religious experience, combined with the needs of the Gentile mission, brought him to the point of regarding the law as a dispensation which had served its purpose, as a *præparatio Evangelica*, " a schoolmaster to bring us to Christ." For him the death of Christ was at once the fulfilment and the abrogation of the law The Christian by the symbolic act of baptism " died to the law " ; he was no longer " under law " but " under grace." The dispensation of the letter gave place to the dispensation of the Spirit.

But the most characteristic thing in Paul's attitude, and yet the least understood, is the eschatological setting of his whole system of belief.

The spirit is the key-note of Paul's thinking. On the one hand, the risen and glorified Christ is identified with the Spirit ; on the other the Spirit, which is the source of all the displays of power and new life that mark the beginnings of the movement, is the first-fruits and pledge of the New Age of the prophets. By virtue of his possession of the Spirit the believer is already in the new age while still living in the old.

So far does Paul carry this belief as to assert that the presence of the Spirit is actually quickening the mortal body of the believer to an ultimate transformation into a spiritual body. The Christian community is living in a brief transition state. The old order where law and sin exist is about to pass away; meanwhile the believer lives already in the new age—he is " in Christ," all things are become new, and shortly the Parousia of Christ will bring in the consummation.

To grasp this outlook of Paul's is to understand how much that now seems to us an arid wilderness of theological dialectic was flashing then with all the hues of the rainbow of a supernatural hope. The dry, theological terms of righteousness, sanctification, predestination were for Paul the glowing facts of Divine energy already transforming the desert of human nature into a beauty which had not entered into the heart of man.

It is difficult to imagine how much of his own vision Paul succeeded in imparting to those communities to whom he pours out his heart in the extraordinary letters which remain to us. There is no doubt that the fruits of the Spirit of which he spoke flourished in many an out-of-the-way place in Asia Minor and Greece. But even in Paul's letters we can see the weeds springing up. The liberty of the Spirit was a heady wine for many. To this day no vessel has been made that will hold it.

But this at least may be said, that Paul was the real spiritual heir of Jesus. One was free-born, the other only won freedom through a struggle bitter as death ; but the Pharisee, in one moment of blinding insight, when all his past fell about him in ruins, saw the spiritual splendour of the faith of a man who had died for love of man, for love of him, to make the dreams of the prophets come true. That faith entered into him, so that the profoundest thing he ever said about himself was that he lived by the faith of the Son of God, who had loved him and given himself for him. Apocalyptic hopes may wither and die, creeds may stand along the dreary road of the church's history as monuments of a dead faith, but in the words of Paul lives the imperishable spirit of courage and love and true freedom.

CHAPTER V

ADJUSTMENT TO THE NEW ENVIRONMENT

THE momentous change which the Christian movement underwent in passing from Jerusalem to Antioch was a change of environment. It passed from a Jewish outlook to a Greek atmosphere and background.

It is only possible to summarize briefly here the main factors in this new environment, bearing in mind that the factors indicated varied in influence according to districts and the various grades of society affected by the Christian movement.

(i) It came into more direct contact with imperial organization. It was obliged to formulate its relationship to the Empire from a political point of view. As a rudimentary organization it found forms of association—even the titles of officials—ready at hand to suggest the outlines and official terminology of its own growing order. In Acts and in Paul's letters the earliest relationship to the Empire is reflected. The Empire is a divinely appointed institution to which Christians owe respect and obedience. It is the restraining influence which hinders the coming of the lawlessness that marks the last days. The whole attitude of Acts is friendly. The change which we find in Revelation and in

1 Peter, the struggle between Church and State, has not yet begun.

(ii) As it made its way among the more educated classes of the Empire the new movement met with various streams of philosophical thought, descendants of the Stoa and the Academy, and was obliged to adjust itself to an element of thought that was wholly absent from its Jewish origin. But this adjustment belongs to a later date. We find its beginnings in Justin Martyr in the middle of the second century. Paul's attitude to philosophy is wholly hostile. "To the Greek foolishness" represents his sense of the philosopher's contempt of the new religion.

(iii) But by far the most important element in the religious environment of the new movement was the widespread existence in the Empire, above all in Asia Minor, of Oriental mystery cults. For a full account of their character and importance the reader may refer to Cumont's "Oriental Religions in Roman Paganism." There is also a good summary in Professor Gardner's "The Religious Experience of St Paul"

The religion of the Olympians was practically dead as a religious force, though it continued to exist as a social and municipal factor. Emperor worship was a political experiment, an attempt to create religious unity and solidarity within the Empire, but it had no religious dynamic behind it. The religious needs of the time were mainly centred in the activities of many forms of a cultus which adhered to one general type. Each of these mystery cults gathered round the figure of a divine Saviour, a god or mythical hero who had died and risen. These cults possessed the common feature of a sacramental initiation, usually some form of baptism, by which the worshipper or initiate was united with the god in death and renewal of life. By the sacrament of initiation the worshipper was assured of forgiveness of sin, of participation in the life of the God, and of a happy immortality.

The process of adjustment of the new movement to this vital factor in the new environment brought about far-reaching changes in both the thought and language of primitive Christianity. In Paul's letters we can see the beginnings of this adjustment.

CHAPTER VI

SALVATION AND ITS MEANING

THE kind of salvation which the earliest preaching offered is summed up in the words of the little Apocalypse in Mark xiii: "He that endureth to the end the same shall be saved." Luke has expressed the same thought more explicitly in his version of the same discourse: "Watch continually, praying that you may have strength to escape all the things that are about to happen and to stand before the Son of man" (Luke xxi. 36). Paul himself never abandoned this apocalyptic view of salvation. In his letter to the Philippians, one of his latest, if not the last, he says: "Our citizenship is in heaven, from whence also we await as Saviour the Lord Jesus who shall transform the body of our humiliation into the likeness of his own body of glory."

Few Jewish minds could escape from this view of the end, but to a Greek it was strange and meaningless. The title "Messiah" in its Greek dress, χριστός, also meant nothing. The title "Lord," κύριος, which seems to have been given to Jesus very early, probably first in Antioch, was, on the other hand, quite familiar, and directly associated both with the mystery cults and with the cult of the emperor. In the same way the title "Saviour," Σωτήρ, was directly connected with the central figures of these cults and with the type of salvation which they were believed to offer to their initiates. Hence the new message of salvation through

Salvation and its Meaning

the death of one whom his messengers called the Lord Jesus or the Lord Jesus Christ, with its accompanying rites of baptism and a sacramental meal, inevitably suggested to the Greek the familiar Lord Serapis, or Mithra, and the rites connected with such cults.

"Christ" ceased to be a Jewish title and became a proper name, and the Lord Jesus or the Lord Jesus Christ, the Saviour, appeared to the pagan seeking for deliverance and healing and for hope in darkness as the central divine figure in a new mystery religion. To him the title Son of God, so often used by Paul, suggested such a mediatorial relationship to the Supreme God as Mithra or Osiris bore to the high gods.

When Paul speaks of dying with Christ by baptism, and of rising to a new life, when he speaks of union with the body of Christ symbolized by participation in the sacramental meal, he was using language consciously adapted to the modes of thought of the Greek familiar with the mystery cults, and his language was bound to be interpreted under those forms. As a Jew, Paul himself was prevented by his Jewish eschatology from adopting a completely sacramental view of the nature of salvation and the relation of the believer to Christ, but his language, the result of the attempt to interpret the Jewish message to the Greek mind, lent itself inevitably to the sacramental implications that arose from the entry of the Christian message into this new environment. In passing from Jerusalem to Antioch the message of the Jesus who had become Messiah by resurrection, and who was about to return to fulfil the promises of God to the prophets, to set up the New Age, and to judge the world, became the message of a Divine Lord and Saviour, Son of God, who had died and risen, and whose sacramental rites offered to the participant forgiveness of sins, new life, and immortality.

It was the beginning of a long process of adaptation and absorption which has caused Christianity to be called sometimes in a good sense, sometimes in a bad one, a syncretistic religion.

Now here it may be remarked that all religions with any vitality, that have not been merely ethical systems, have been syncretistic in proportion to their vitality. Hebrew religion had always been syncretistic, that is, had been able to absorb elements from its religious environment; its law and mythology were largely Babylonian, its eschatology and angelology were mainly Persian, and it only ceased to be syncretistic when it became, under the influence of Rabbinical methods, an almost wholly ethical religion. The essence of religion lies in the fact that it is the embodiment, in practices and beliefs, of the desires of men—desires which range from the desire for good crops and fertile cattle to the desire for immortality. Hence while these desires and the forms in which they are embodied may be, and have been, rationalized into theological systems, yet they are not themselves based on reason and evidence, but on emotion.

There is no such thing as syncretism in science, because its basis is not desire but knowledge and critically examined evidence. But a religion, as long as it has power to satisfy the desires of man, is also capable of absorbing into itself, without producing a sense of incongruity or incompatibility, current beliefs and practices which embody the desires of those to whom it comes.

But there were other elements which Paul's message contained, less familiar, intelligible, and acceptable to the pagan convert. We can see from his letters to Corinth and Thessalonica that in the first place his Jewish eschatology was difficult to understand and met with considerable scepticism, and in the second place his high ethical standards were somewhat irksome to those who found his theory of freedom from the law more to their liking than his insistence on hard work, continence, and brotherly love. Nevertheless, these two elements passed into the life and creed of the early Church. Although Paul's belief in the Parousia was weakened by the passage of time and eventually passed into a vague expectation of a return to judgment embodied in the creeds, yet his belief in a bodily resurrection, as against Greek ideas, passed into the creeds, possibly because of its value to the Church as a hold upon the ordinary believer through its connexion with the belief in future material reward and punishment.

In the same way Paul's Jewish ethics, the highest ethics known to the pagan world, became the standard of the Christian life, again probably through the need that the Church felt in its struggle with the Empire to display the highest standards of good citizenship and social ethics. The Empire could only find charges against the Church on political, never on moral, grounds.

CHAPTER VII

GROWTH OF CHRISTOLOGY AND ORGANIZATION

BEFORE passing on to the third stage of development there are two points that call for some consideration.

The first is Paul's own working out of the problem of the personality of Jesus. While, as we have already seen, the main factor in the growth of the new conception lay in the changed environment, yet Paul's own thinking came in later to supplement and reinforce the new conception. It is more than probable that the problem of the relation between the Messiah of apocalyptic expectation and his own personal nature underlay a good deal of the experience of Jesus. Although it is impossible to dogmatize on the point, yet there are strong grounds for supposing that Jesus believed that his manifestation as Messiah or Son of man would follow upon his death and resurrection. That resurrection would effect the change from the human personality as son of Joseph, which he knew himself to be, to the supernatural personality of Son of man, which he believed himself appointed by God to become. But whether Jesus believed this or not, the early preaching suggests that the disciples believed that he had been elevated to the position of Messiah through resurrection. Perhaps the simplest form of theological statement representing this belief is found in the first chapter of the First Epistle of Peter, verses 20, 21,

Growth of Christology 113

χριστοῦ προεγνωσμένου μὲν . . . φανερωθέντος δέ, foreknown and manifested, then raised and glorified. But the relation between Jesus of Nazareth and the Foreknown Messiah is left undefined.

For Paul the peculiar sharpness of the experience that convinced him that the Nazarene was the Messiah raised the problem more insistently. As a Pharisee he believed in the pre-existence of the Messiah, certainly not in the Catholic sense of pre-existence, but in the sense that Messiah, like the law, was created before the world, and was to be revealed at God's appointed time. The identification of Jesus the Nazarene with this supernatural pre-existent heavenly Messiah led Paul to certain conclusions. He believed that through resurrection the actual identification had been effected, the earthly Jesus had become the heavenly Messiah, the quickening Lord, the Spirit. But there is no suggestion that the earthly Jesus was in any sense pre-existent. The only passage in Paul's letters which is capable of such an interpretation is Phil. ii. 6–11. This passage, like others in Paul's letters, could easily be used in support of the belief in the pre-existence of the human Jesus when once that belief had established itself in the Church, but is capable of an interpretation which limits the pre-existence to the Messiah, and suggests the exaltation of Jesus to the Messiahship: "Given him the name," etc. (For further discussion of verses 6–8, see Note on p. 118).

Paul's problem was really threefold:

(i) He had to explain how the historical Jesus could be identified with the heavenly Messiah. His answer was, through resurrection; and the result was that his emphasis was almost entirely on the risen Christ, not on the Christ "after the flesh."

(ii) He had to explain the depth and intensity of the religious experience which resulted from his acceptance of this identification. His answer was that Jesus had become a quickening spirit, the Spirit of God, and dwelt in him and in all who accepted the Messiahship and Lordship of Jesus, becoming thus the source of power and joy and all spiritual gifts.

(iii) He had to explain the relation between this identification and consequent experience, and the great apocalyptic change which he expected. His answer was, first, that the resurrection and change of Jesus from corporeal to spiritual existence was the first act in the apocalyptic drama ; second, that those in whom the spirit of Jesus dwelt were already partakers of the life of the age to come ; third, that the Parousia, shortly expected, would complete the consummation and bring in the New Age.

This was Paul's working out of the relation of Jesus to his own beliefs in a supernatural Messiah and an apocalyptic world order, but most of it came to be interpreted later in support of a wholly different system of thought.

The second point is the question of how far organization had developed by the time of Paul's death.

The subject is highly controversial and needs a book rather than a chapter to deal with it. Here I can only suggest certain general results as a starting point.

Growth of Christology

First of all, the history or organization in Jerusalem must be considered apart from the growth of organized communities in the Græco-Roman world, and while the authority of the Jerusalem community had undoubtedly considerable weight in the early years of expansion, yet the strictly Jewish character of the community there and its dispersion after A.D. 70 rendered its permanent influence on the growth of the church organization very slight.

Second, we can trace three distinct stages up to the middle of the second century :

(i) The period of " enthusiasm," to use Harnack's phrase, during which the Parousia was regarded as imminent and the gifts of the Spirit were regarded as " the powers of the age to come." A certain amount of regulation was necessary, as Paul's letters show, but any organization was purely temporary and *ad hoc* until Christ himself should set up the Kingdom, when the saints would reign and judge.

(ii) The period during which the Parousia hope was fading and the new movement was spreading all over Asia Minor and the Empire. The new communities probably assumed various forms of organization modelled on the local forms with which they were familiar. They were independent and self-governing, although maintaining close relations with neighbouring communities by means of letters and messengers.

(iii) The period of State hostility, beginning with the Neronian and continuing under the Flavian persecutions, began to weld the communities into a whole. The necessity of distinguishing themselves from the Jews, as well as the necessity of making clear lines of demarcation between themselves and the many similar communities which rapidly sprung up, created the machinery of the monarchical episcopate to interpret the tradition in a uniform way and to maintain discipline. It became necessary to define conditions of membership, terms of belief, and the number of sacred books in a way which should be valid for the whole body of Christian communities.

In Paul's letters we can see the characteristics of the first two periods. For Paul everything is in view of the end. The time is short. All human and social institutions have only a temporary value. But, on the other hand, the " new things " have begun, and already the gifts of the Spirit manifest themselves in various ways in different individuals. The regulative principles which Paul recognizes are love, which seeks to exercise these gifts for the good of all, and holiness, which should mark out the " people of God " from " this present evil world."

We can see from Paul's letters, especially the Corinthian letters, that no very definite organization for discipline or ritual existed. The weekly meetings must have been very disorderly, the central rite of the Lord's Supper, as far as we can gather from 1 Cor. xi., was not clearly separated from the communal meal. There seems to have been a rivalry in the display of " gifts," which produced a disorder most distasteful to a mind accustomed to the decorum of a synagogue. But there is no suggestion of the existence of a responsible official, or body of officials, who are worthy of

Growth of Christology

praise or blame for the condition of the community. The contrast with the letters of Ignatius in this respect is very great.

The letter to the community at Philippi includes bishops and deacons in its opening salutation, but no mention of their duties occurs in the letter, and it would seem that the stage of the single bishop assisted by a body of presbyters had not yet been reached at Philippi. In the neighbouring community of Thessalonica, Paul refers to the existence of " those who are over you " (τοὺς προϊσταμένους ὑμῶν), and begs that such be recognized and valued for their work. Acts refers to the elders of the community at Ephesus, and represents Paul as saying to them in his farewell address that the Holy Spirit had made them bishops in the flock, and as charging them to shepherd the ecclesia of God. Likewise, at the end of the first missionary journey Paul and Barnabas are said to have appointed (χειροτονέω) elders in the various South Galatian communities.

Hence the evidence suggests that officials existed, probably appointed by apostolic authority, in most, if not all, of the Gentile Christian communities. Nevertheless, they are not regarded as central in the life of the community. Paul does not address his letters to them with instructions for the order and discipline of the community. The most important thing seems to be the exercise of " gifts," of which " prophecy " is esteemed the most highly by Paul. For Paul the present needs of the ecclesia are met by the Divine appointment of gifts, beginning with apostles as the foundation " gift," and including every variety of spiritual manifestation. At this stage the charismatic ministry completely overshadowed the official, although the latter existed in germ and in time took the place of the former.

In Jerusalem and the Palestinian communities it is probable that the synagogue furnished the model of organization. The important passage relating to discipline in Matt. xviii. reflects the influence of synagogue methods of discipline and probably depicts the state of the Palestinian Christian communities in the last quarter of the first century.

Note (on Phil. ii. 6-8).

This passage has always been one of the principal supports for the view that Paul held a thoroughgoing pre-existent doctrine of the Person of Christ, but this view turns largely on the translation of the passage, and the translation has undoubtedly been influenced by the view that it is made to support.

The interpretation turns on the meaning of ἁρπαγμός, μορφή, and ἴσος.

The passage should be taken in its context. It is an argument directed to influence the conduct of the Philippians by the example of Jesus. Paul desires that the same disposition (τοῦτο φρονεῖτε) should be displayed by them that was manifest in the conduct of Jesus. Hence we should expect μορφή and ἴσος to have a moral significance, as they usually do in Paul's letters, rather than a metaphysical one. Also the distinction between ἁρπαγμός and ἅρπαγμα should be preserved. The passage might then be paraphrased: " Let your disposition resemble that of Christ Jesus, who since he was morally like God did not consider that moral likeness to God consisted in seeking one's own advantage, but rather divested himself of what was due to him (i.e. as Messiah) etc." The result being that God exalted him to the highest place. This is clearly not pre-existent but adoptionist Christology, yet it is obvious that the ambiguity of language lent itself very easily to a pre-existent interpretation.

PART IV

THE CHURCH IN THE EMPIRE

CHAPTER I

MAIN CURRENTS OF INFLUENCE

THE history of Christianity has suffered much from misleading metaphors. None perhaps has presented a falser view than the metaphor of the seed, which contains the whole potentiality of later development within itself. Far truer is the analogy of the stream, which in its descent into the plains receives tributaries from various other sources and carries down with it all kinds of elements collected in its course.

Perhaps equally unfortunate is the attempt to characterize the earliest period of enthusiasm as the only genuine Christianity, and to seek to return to a period whose state of mind and outlook is so foreign to our present state of development as to be almost unintelligible save to the trained historical imagination.

The truth is that the history of the religious movement called Christianity is the history of the interaction of many widely different currents of thought and social forces, the original impulse forming only one of these various currents.

We have to consider now the effect of various fresh currents of thought, and of fresh social forces, upon the movement whose development we have traced so far.

First of all, a summary of the main factors will make clear the problems involved; then we can proceed to deal with each in turn as fully as space will permit.

We have to understand, first of all, the beginnings of what may be called self-consciousness in the new movement. This appears in various directions. The Christian community embodied in its far-flung churches from one end of the Empire to the other by the close of the first century had begun to realize that it stood facing the Empire. As a heavenly state of society it challenged the whole earthly order embodied in the Empire. The book of Revelation expresses this consciousness very clearly and sharply, and expresses also the extraordinary sense of triumph, the sense that the scaffold sways the future. The friendly and politic attitude of Acts has disappeared and the Empire is the dragon, many-headed, the enemy of the man-child, the Lamb slain, who is to rule the nations with a rod of iron. The persecuted Church is the Lamb's bride. Over against Rome, the harlot, gleams the heavenly bride of the Lamb, the new Jerusalem, arrayed in the glory of God.

Secondly, the new community had now consciously outgrown its Jewish origin and stood definitely challenging the Jewish race and its claims. Paul had claimed that Christ was the end of the law, but while he could say that in Christ there was neither Jew nor Greek, he never forgot that he was a Jew. But there is a peculiar irony in the attitude of the Christian Church in its new self-consciousness. It claims to be the true Israel, the true heir of the promises; it takes over the Jewish Scriptures and places its own newer documents alongside of them as the Divine revelation of the Old and New Covenants together committed by

God to the guardianship and interpretation of the Church. The Jews are dismissed as apostates, even as impostors who claim what does not belong to them. The Old Testament is ransacked to furnish prophecies of the details of the life and death of Jesus. The Old Testament is the shadow of which the new order is the reality.

Thirdly, this dawning self-consciousness expresses itself in competition with the philosophy of the Græco-Roman world. The need is felt of some explicit statement of the cosmic significance of Christ and the Church. We find the beginnings of that Christian philosophy which is worked out so fully by Clement of Alexandria and Origen, although its ultimate influence on the masses and on the formulation of Church doctrine was not so important. But its most important effect, apart from the attraction which it exercised upon educated converts to Christianity, lay in its shaping of the doctrine of the personality of Christ and his significance in the universe. Through the impact of philosophy upon Christianity we have the identification of Jesus with the Stoic Logos, the Divine reason immanent in the universe, explaining both its origin and its order.

Fourthly, the external pressure upon the Church of the many competing forms of Oriental cults, half mystic philosophies, half sacramental mystery cults, together commonly grouped under the convenient term Gnosticism, produced a number of important results :

(i) The Church presented itself increasingly to the masses as an institution which possessed and could impart salvation through its sacred mysteries. The old eschatological conception of the powers of the Spirit as an earnest of the New Age became concentrated in the channels of the Sacraments. Through baptism and the Lord's Supper the participant received the Divine nature and immortality. This idea of apotheosis, which satisfied one of the deepest demands of the religious need of the age, becomes more and more prominent in the writings of the early Fathers.

(ii) The officials of the Church assumed a new character, partly due to its Jewish antecedents, but far more due to the influence of the mystery cults. They became priests, celebrants of the sacred mysteries, a class possessing peculiar powers and privileges. The clergy began to stand out against the laity as a priestly caste.

(iii) The growth of a mass of apocryphal literature and the efflorescence of all kinds of speculation in which the figure of Jesus was involved made it necessary for the Church to lay down the limits of the canon, to select those documents which it was prepared to accept as authoritative. It was, moreover, obliged to formulate in brief the outline of what was to be believed, the *regula fidei*, the beginnings of authoritative creed. Finally, it was obliged to assert for itself the possession, in the hands of the priestly caste, of the true tradition in accordance with which the accepted Scriptures must be interpreted.

But through these various changes, producing so great a transformation of the primitive group in

Jerusalem, one thing remains fixed, Christ is central. It is true that the figure of Jesus also has suffered a great transformation, but the Church holds fast in theory and in experience to the central fact that a historical figure is the spring and source of all.

This is the key-note of all the literature of the first three centuries. While we can see in Cyprian, Lactantius, and other Latin fathers the tendency to make the Church central—a tendency which is completely realized in the Mediaeval Church (save for the continual stream of mystical devotion attached to the person of Christ)—yet at first, in this earlier period, Christ is first and the Church second.

While this is true, it is also true that the Christ who is the central object of devotion and of theological speculation is not the Jesus of history. The inner necessity of harmonizing the historical figure with the results of the transformation caused by the factors we have discussed led to rationalizing speculations which issued finally in the compromise of the Tome of Leo and the Chalcedonian definition in the fifth century, a position from which we are only now beginning to break loose.

CHAPTER II

JESUS AND GOD

ONE of the important results of the Jewish origin of the Christian movement was that when that movement met the flux of religious thought in the society of the time it brought with it and held fast to a clearly defined personal idea of God. Nothing of the work of the Hebrew prophets was lost. Almost every form of belief or non-belief in God that has ever influenced men's minds and actions was current in the first century of the Christian era. Through it all the Church held fast to the belief in a personal God with definite personal attributes, with a definite plan for the course of the world and for the individual.

It was the necessity of explaining the relation of the central figure of Jesus to this God that gave its direction to the main stream of Christian thinking for the first five centuries of its history.

The original Jewish-Christian position was simple. Jesus was the man who had been selected by God as the Messiah. The resurrection was a supernatural act which had ratified and made effectual the position of Jesus. He was in Heaven waiting to return and set up the Kingdom of Jewish expectation.

As we have seen, this position had little or no meaning to the minds of Gentile hearers of the new message. The message underwent a transformation into the terms of the mystery-cults with which they were familiar, and which expressed their religious needs. The primitive Messiah became the divine Lord and Saviour. Here, in connexion with the new self-consciousness of which we have spoken, arose the need of explaining the relation of this divine Lord to God. Two lines of explanation, both connected with contemporary tendencies of thought, and both reflected in the early Christian literature, are apparent. One of them, as we shall see, ultimately ousted the other.

The first, which is related in some ways to the Jewish form of thought, and in others to the Greek idea of heroes or demi-gods, was the conception of apotheosis, of a man who through merit became God.

We can trace this line of thought from the early preaching in Acts, where Jesus is declared to have been made Lord and Messiah by God, through Paul, who speaks of Jesus as born of the seed of David but marked out (ὁρισθέντος) Son of God by resurrection through endowment with the Spirit of God, to its most striking statement in the Shepherd of Hermas, a document which comes from the Roman Church about the first quarter of the second century. Those who wish can consult the text of Hermas in Lightfoot's "Apostolic Fathers," or in Professor Lake's excellent edition of the Apostolic Fathers in Loeb's Classical Library.

Hermas represents God the Father taking counsel with the Spirit, who is the Son, as to what reward Jesus the Servant who has perfectly fulfilled his earthly service is deserving of. They decide to elevate him to divine Sonship. While details are uncertain, the general line of thought is unmistakable. It represents what has been called the Adoptionist explanation of the relation of Jesus to God.

On the one hand, this explanation guards Jewish monotheism to some extent, and on the other favours the idea of apotheosis, the possibility of man becoming God, towards which men's desires were so strongly turning at this time.

The second line of explanation has also relations to elements in both Jewish and Greek thought. It is the opposite conception of God becoming man, involving the idea of the pre-existence of Jesus. Now this conception was related on the one hand to the Jewish idea of the pre-existence of the Messiah, which we have already mentioned, and on the other lends itself readily both to the Stoic conception of the Logos Spermatikos and to Gnostic Oriental conceptions of emanations or Æons.

The Fourth Gospel represents the earliest form of this explanation. Jesus is the pre-existent Word, the Logos who was with God in the beginning. The Word became flesh. Jesus comes from God and goes to God. The human life of Jesus, while perfectly real, is only an episode in the eternal existence of the Son with the Father.

This line of explanation, which, owing to the traditional connexion of the Fourth Gospel with Ephesus, we may call the Ephesian in contrast with the Roman Adoptionist explanation, was the one which ultimately gained universal acceptance, though not without much protest, in the Church.

CHAPTER III

THE FOURTH GOSPEL AND ITS INFLUENCE

THERE can be little doubt that the acceptance of the Fourth Gospel by the Church determined the issue of the central problem. There were many reasons why the Adoptionist answer to the question what is meant by the term " Son of God " should have met with wide acceptance. It softened the break with polytheism, it allied itself naturally with the mystery-cults, it was less abstract and philosophical than the pre-existent view, and the subsequent history of Arianism and the tendencies of the Antiochene School of theologians shows how hard it was to eradicate this view. Indeed, it has never been wholly banished, but has lingered unwelcome and suspect on the confines of orthodoxy. It is probably stronger to-day in the Church than it has ever been since the days of the Arian Emperors.

Neither is there any valid reason for denying that the religious experience connected with this belief is less satisfying and vital than the experience arising from the pre-existent belief.

But the Fourth Gospel was a work of supreme genius, and when once, in the face of much opposition, it was accepted by the Church, the earlier lives of Jesus, together with Paul's Christology, were interpreted in the sense of the Fourth Gospel.

It became the touchstone of orthodoxy and the poin

of departure for the fresh development of the doctrine of the relation of Jesus to God.

There are three main elements in the Fourth Gospel to which it owed its pre-eminence over the earlier tendencies in the Church. First, it provided the formula of the Logos, a conception which may have arisen from an earlier Christian identification of Jesus with the Wisdom of God, as Professor Rendel Harris has proved with such abundance of learning in his " Prologue to St. John's Gospel," but which certainly lent itself to Stoic ideas of the immanent Reason and to later Neo-Platonic conceptions of the Logos Prophorikos, the outgoing energy of the Divine Reason personified and active in creation, serving as the necessary link between God and the world.

Secondly, though not perhaps logically consistent with the Logos idea, the Fourth Gospel offers a thoroughly sacramental conception of the relation between Jesus and the believer. Life is obtained through eating the flesh of the Son of man and drinking his blood. He is the bread of God coming down from Heaven. Here satisfaction was offered to the religious need that sought expression in the mystery-cults. Christianity was conceived of as a mystery-cult of the profoundest and most spiritual kind.

Thirdly, the Fourth Gospel removed the stumbling-block of Apocalyptic. There were only two ways of dealing with Apocalyptic. The Book of Revelation shows one way—a way which has always been attractive to many heroic souls. It is the way of a reaffirmation. As each crisis of history passes and it appears that the End is not yet, no final victory is won, the prophetic soul projects the vision still further into the future, and paints it in brighter colours in reaction from each bitter disappointment.

But the author of the Fourth Gospel showed the way of escape from the crude determinism and the time-schemes of current apocalyptic thought into the timeless realm of the Spirit. For the vision of a world-shaking judgment and the final triumph of the martyred saints with the Lamb slain he substituted the perpetual triumph of love stronger than death, and of the faith that overcomes the world.

We do not know how the Fourth Gospel reached Rome from Ephesus. It is an attractive suggestion and in accordance with historical probability that Justin Martyr brought the Ephesian Christology to Rome. It was new and had obvious dangers. It lent itself to the Docetic tendencies so widely current at the time, in spite of its insistence on the reality of the humanity of Jesus, and hence it met with much opposition at Rome. But by the time of Irenæus its place in the Canon was so assured that for Irenæus the fourfold Gospel scheme is part of the Divine plan. Not only so, but its Christology determined the history of the Church's doctrine of Christ, and the Adoptionist explanation became a heresy. Nevertheless, one element in Adoptionism was too strong to be rejected —the thought that through participation in the Christian mysteries the initiate became a " Son of God." Even as late as the fourth century Athanasius, the great protagonist of the pre-existent Christology, in his famous phrase, αὐτὸς γὰρ ἐνανθρώπησεν ἵνα ἡμεῖς θεοποιηθῶμεν—" He became man that we might be made God "—shows the persistence of this element which is so marked in Paul and in the letter to the Hebrews. But it was not really compatible in its full sense with the pre-existent explanation and gradually became weakened, until in mediaeval and later popular Christian thought it was reduced to the idea that Christians became angels after death.

As the product, then, of a profound religious experience and of a great spiritual genius the Fourth Gospel provided at the same time a ground for mystical experience independent of historical limitations, freedom from apocalyptic schemes, and a starting-point for a Christian metaphysic and philosophy of history.

CHAPTER IV

THE EPISCOPATE AND ITS WORK

BUT neither the life of Jesus, the work of Paul, nor the appearance of the Fourth Gospel and its acceptance by the Church at the beginning of the first century will explain the rise and progress of the great unified institution that dominates the course of history from Constantine to Innocent III.

The real cause of the survival of the Christian movement, its triumph over many kindred movements, and its consolidation into a great institution lay elsewhere.

It is impossible to describe here in detail the evolution of the monarchical episcopate, and many of its early details are still matters of dispute. But the outstanding fact is that the loose union of scattered churches with a charismatic ministry gradually gives way to a quasi-military organization on a territorial basis following the Roman provincial and parochial organization.

There were two main external factors that brought about this decisive change in the organization of the Church. The first was the external pressure of the various forms of sects and cults, all containing elements of Christian tradition mingled with Oriental speculation and varied forms of ritual practices borrowed from the mystery-cults. All were agreed that the original impulse of the Christian movement sprang from the words and life of the historical Jesus, but the flood of allegorical interpretation which had already invaded Jewish religion threatened to submerge all historical landmarks and to deprive nascent Christianity of any fixed meaning.

The need of fixing the content of Christianity led to the establishment of a body of permanent officials whose office it was so determine and safeguard the deposit of truth. In every locality the bishop became the guardian of the faith. It was the work of the bishops to determine three fundamental things:

(i) The limits of the canon of Scripture.
(ii) The nature and contents of the *regula fidei*—the rule of faith, what was to be believed.
(iii) The contents of the apostolic tradition, transmitted from the apostles to the bishops, in accordance with which the Scriptures and the rule of faith must be interpreted.

All the various so-called Gnostic sects and schools claimed the right to accept or reject any of the rapidly multiplying sacred books at their pleasure. Marcion had his own canon. The various Gnostic schools had their own collections of apocryphal Gospels and Acts, their own methods of allegorical interpretation, their own secret tradition of gnosis.

In the face of this universal flux, which threatened to reduce the Christian movement to one among a thousand little esoteric schools of religious belief and practice, the evolution of the episcopal order during the first two centuries resulted in the fixing of canon, creed, and tradition with sufficient definiteness to become the basis of the Catholic conception of Vincent of Lerinum and Augustine, the *quod semper, quod ubique, quod ab omnibus*.

The second main factor was the situation that arose

The Episcopate and its Work

after the outbreak of persecution under Decius in the middle of the third century. The thoroughness and unexpectedness of the attack, coming after a long period of toleration, produced an unusually large number of the "lapsi," i.e. those who bowed to the storm and conformed nominally to paganism. As soon as the persecution ceased the question of readmission arose. The centre of the struggle was at Carthage, where Cyprian had to contend, on the one hand, against the promiscuous use of the privilege of "confessors" to grant restoration to the lapsed, and on the other against the rigorists, who wished to exclude for ever from the Church all who had fallen. The dispute shifted to Rome, where the puritan party elected Novatian as bishop in opposition to the election of Cornelius by the party which stood for charity to the lapsed. This raised the vital question, for the administrative unity of the Church, whether it was possible to have two bishops in the one locality. The letters of Cyprian vividly represent the keenness of the controversy. Cyprian's views prevailed, and it was henceforth accepted that there could only be one bishop in a local church even as there was only one God. But the struggle lasted for many years.

Nevertheless, the principle was established that the bishop represented the unity of the Church for discipline as well as for doctrine. The result of this development was an important and far-reaching change in the conception of the bishop's character and functions.

In the letters of Ignatius, at the beginning of the second century, we find repeatedly the statement that the bishop in the community represents God the Father, or Christ, while the presbyters represent the apostles.

But the result of the struggle against Gnosticism and of the Novatianist schism was that the bishop came to be regarded as occupying the Apostles' seat and power. Hence gradually it was accepted that the bishop was the sole possessor of the power of binding and loosing entrusted to the Apostles and the channel of the various gifts of the Spirit.

Henceforward, while the stream of inner experience flowed on, the history of the Church is the history of the struggle between the great Sees, of Synods and Councils, of belief and practice which are not the spontaneous expression of inward experience but the result of compromise and adjustment in the clash of ecclesiastical politics. The Christian Church had ceased to be a movement and had become an institution.

CHAPTER V

THE COMPLETION OF THE CHRISTOLOGY

WE have already seen that the Church inherited from its Jewish origin the central doctrine of one personal God, with various personal attributes.

The acceptance of the pre-existent explanation of the personality of Jesus created a problem which occupied the theologians of the Church for five centuries.

Two main stages of this problem appear. The first was concerned with the difficulty of reconciling the oneness of God with the admission that Jesus was God. The solution, if such it can be called, to the first stage of the problem was the evolution of the idea of the Trinity to which Roman law and Greek metaphysics contributed. The mystery of the three Persons and one Substance was the formula accepted to express the nature of God. The Catholic formula steered the middle course between the Scylla of tritheism and the Charybdis of an economic Trinity, a threeness which was not really threeness but the dynamic manifestation of one energy in three forms. The only refuge for the faithful lay in the acceptance of a mystery which transcended human reason, ignoring the fact that human reason had created the mystery.

The second stage of the problem, far more acute, was concerned with the difficulty of reconciling the fact that Jesus was an historical person with the theory of his pre-existence. How could he be both God and man at the same time ? How could he be born in time and yet eternally pre-existent ?

The solution, like the previous one, had to avoid the danger of denying his real humanity on the one hand, and on the other of reducing his divinity to that of an inferior deity, as Arianism did, or of denying any substantial union of divinity and humanity in his person. The answer was an illogical compromise, the so-called Two-natures hypothesis stated finally by the Roman Church in the Tome of Leo in the fifth century. Like the Trinity, the formula of " God and Man one Christ " could only be accepted as a mystery which transcended human comprehension and must be accepted by faith for salvation.

So Jesus disappeared into the keeping of the theologians. The schism between the East and West, the conquest of the West by barbarism, the accession of the Roman Church to the prestige of the Roman Empire, the interposition of the Moslem barrier between the East and West, are the main factors in the subsequent development. The Church presents the appearance of Paul's ship aground at Melita, " the fore-part stuck fast, the hinder-part was broken by the violence of the waves."

In the West the monarchical episcopate developed into the papacy and Roman supremacy, achieved the spiritual conquest of the barbarians, preserved alive the tradition of culture, and built up a catholicism of doctrine and practice in which countless souls found peace and fulfilment of their spirit's quest. It was a great and splendid achievement.

In the East, where Rome's claim to spiritual supremacy had never been accepted and where the subtler mind of the Greek, in Alexandria or Antioch, had

The Completion of the Christology

continued to speculate on the central problems of Christianity, no such catholic unity was achieved. The Arab conquest destroyed the Eastern empire, as the Goths did the Western; but the Arabs were not conquered by the religion of the conquered, as were the Goths. Instead, the Church was broken up into various competing sects and churches, with varying forms of theological belief, many of which still survive.

The vision of the Nazarene has had a strange issue. His saying, " I came not to bring peace but a sword," has received an unexpected fulfilment.

EPILOGUE

A RECENT writer on Sociology has thus summed up the situation whose development we have attempted to trace :

The particular combination of the tradition of a great teacher with elements drawn from ancient mythology and contemporary East Mediterranean religion and philosophy, which was formulated at Nicæa in 325 A.D., may now prove to be no more firmly rooted than was the Græco-Roman state religion—in spite of its temples and priesthoods and its intimate connection with men's habits of thought and speech and feeling and education—when Lucian attacked it in the second century A.D. It is true there is evidence which persuades many observers that Christian orthodoxy will maintain or even increase its authority by shedding its mythology and absorbing non-Christian ideas. But a time comes when a religion loses its power of retaining its vitality in a new form; there were indications of a corresponding transformation of the state religion in the times of Marcus Aurelius and of Porphyry, but the transformed faith soon died out. I myself think it more probable that the children or grandchildren of most of those who reject the main dogmas of Christian orthodoxy will cease to call themselves Christians; and that Christian tradition will come to be represented in the Western nations by a minority of born mystics and their followers.

Such is the impression produced upon a scientific observer by the development of the Christian movement seen in its historical perspective. His forecast is, of course, merely an individual speculation, and may be entirely disproved by the future course of events, but the whole passage serves to emphasize the present situation and its most striking features. It presents the sharp contrast between two apparently incompatible views of the universe.

On the one hand Christianity appears as a Divine intervention in the course of human affairs. It is the irruption of the supernatural into the world of men, the supreme event of history, God become man; and His presence in His world, to use Leo's phrase, "coruscates with miracle."

Hence Christianity as a religion is the last word, the absolute religion. It supplies a satisfying philosophy of the universe, a final rule of conduct, an emotional experience which answers the deepest demands of life, and contains the assurance of a blessed immortality.

On the other hand, in the light of the view of the universe which science has slowly built up during the last hundred years the Christian movement represents one stage in the intellectual and emotional development of the West. Its ideas and practices and the form of its institutions are determined partly by its antecedents and partly by its environment. There is no ground for supposing that it is a final stage of human development.

Its philosophy of history and the universe which explains both as the result of a supernatural personal agency does not satisfy modern intellectual needs. While its code of ethics is high it is not necessarily the final form of human conduct. The emotional satisfaction which it yields is not necessarily attached to any particular form of religious belief, as the history of religious experience abundantly proves.

Hence we have a point of view, the result of historical investigation, combined with the acceptance of the broad scientific view of the universe which recognizes the enormous value of Christianity in history, but does not acknowledge its finality nor its supernatural authority.

Canon Scott Holland, shortly before his death, facing this situation, said: "The platitudes on which we have confidently rested break from under us"; and again: "Thought and will must come out into the open and make their venture."

Three attitudes are possible in the face of the situation thus outlined. It is possible to fall back upon authority—the authority of the Bible or the Church. For many this is the way of safety. There is the attitude of Gallio-like indifference. Many will say, indeed are saying, that religion is wholly discredited, and cease to take any interest in its implications for life and conduct. This attitude also is widespread, as it was in the time of the decay of the State religion in the first two centuries of Christianity. There is the third attitude of which Canon Scott Holland speaks. Thought and will may come out into the open and make their venture. This is the hardest way. It involves the scientific attitude of humility before the facts of the universe, not distorting or transfiguring them by desire. It involves the will to recognize and conserve values, to face the fact of the perpetual movement of that mysterious force which we call life.

What the result of that venture of thought and will may be we cannot foresee, any more than Jesus or Paul could forecast the issue of their heroic ventures, their conflict with the binding forces of agelong tradition.

But history proves this at least; that the venture

belongs to the creative force of life, and always yields new forms of experience, makes a new dwelling in which the spirit of man may abide for a time to contemplate the changing yet eternal forms of beauty and truth, before he is forced on to fresh adventure and discovery. This faith is the victory that overcomes the world.

APPENDICES

APPENDIX I

PASSAGES FROM JEWISH APOCALYPTIC LITERATURE ILLUSTRATING BELIEFS CONCERNING THE RESURRECTION

(a) *1 Enoch xxii. 13.*

Such (a division) has been made for the spirits of men who were not righteous but sinners, who were complete in transgression, and of the transgressors they shall be companions: but their spirits shall not be slain in the Day of Judgment nor shall they be raised from thence.

1 Enoch li. 1.

And in those days shall the earth also give back that which has been entrusted to it, and Sheol also shall give back that which it has received, and hell shall give back that which it owes.

1 Enoch lxi. 5.

And these measures shall reveal all the secrets of the depths of the earth, and those who have been destroyed by the desert, and those who have been destroyed by the beasts, and those who have been destroyed by the fish of the sea, that they may return and stay themselves on the day of the Elect One.

1 Enoch xci. 10.

And the righteous shall arise from their sleep, and wisdom shall arise and be given unto them.

(b) *Testimony of Judah xxv. 1, 4.*

And after these things shall Abraham and Isaac and Jacob arise unto life . . . and they who have died in grief shall arise in joy, and they who were poor for the Lord's sake shall be made rich, and they who are put to death for the Lord's sake shall awake to life.

Testimony of Benjamin x. 6, 7.

Then shall ye see Enoch, Noah and Shem, and Abraham and Isaac and Jacob rising on the right hand in gladness. Then shall we also rise, each over our own tribe, and we shall worship the Heavenly King. Then shall we all be changed, some into glory and some into shame (cf. Dan. xii. 1, 2).

(c) 2 Baruch, xxx. 1, 2.

And it shall come to pass after these things, when the time of the advent of the Messiah is fulfilled, that He shall return in glory. Then all who have fallen asleep in hope of Him shall rise again.

2 Baruch, cc. xlix–li.

This is the fullest passage in the Apocalyptic literature and should be consulted by those interested. It presents remarkable parallels to Paul's teaching in 1 Cor. xv. It is too long to be given here in full. In c. xlix. Baruch asks God concerning the resurrection: " In what shape will those live who live in Thy day ? Or how will the splendour of those who are after that time continue ? " He receives the answer from God: " The earth shall then assuredly restore the dead, it shall make no changes in their form, but as it has received so it shall restore them, and as I delivered them unto it, so also shall it raise them. For then it will be necessary to show to the living that the dead have come to life again, and that those who had departed have returned."

The passage goes on to describe the change of the righteous to glory and of the wicked to shame.

These passages are taken from the Oxford edition of the Old Testament Apocrypha and Pseudepigrapha edited by Dr. Charles. The student should refer to the note on 1 Enoch li. 1. For fuller discussion of the growth of Jewish ideas on Resurrection see Charles " Eschatology, Hebrew, Jewish and Christian."

APPENDIX II

Rabbinical Arguments for the Resurrection

In the main the Rabbinical arguments for the Resurrection fall under three heads:

(i) *Inferences from Particular Passages of Scripture.* These inferences are often based on a forced or artificial connection of words. For example, in Deut. xxxi. 16, by separating וְקָם from הָעָם הַזֶּה and connecting it with the previous words, they produced the translation: "Thou shalt sleep with thy fathers and shalt arise," and consequently used the passage as a proof of the resurrection.

Other examples are Cant. vii. 10, where "the lips of them that are asleep" is interpreted as referring to the dead and the inference of resurrection drawn therefrom. Deut. iv. 4 and xi. 9 were similarly used. For a full list of passages so used the student may refer to the valuable note in Strack and Billerbeck's "Commentar Zum Neuen Testament aus Talmud und Midrash on Matt. xxii. 32," pp. 893-897.

(ii) *Inferences from Previous Cases of Resurrection.*—The stories of Elijah and Elisha are of course accepted as historical and used as the basis for further proof of the Resurrection in the Age to come. The story of Ezekiel in the valley of dry bones is also taken literally as a case of Resurrection on a large scale!

(iii) *The General Argument from Analogy.*—This is generally found in Haggadic form. For instance the Haggada in Genesis Rabbah 14 is repeated elsewhere in modified forms. The translation of it will illustrate the general character of this line of proof: "There was a man in Zepphoris whose son died. A heretic went in to sit with him. Rabbi Jose ben Halaphta went up to greet him.

The heretic saw him sitting and laughing. He said to him, 'Why do you laugh?' He replied, 'We trust in the Lord of Heaven that you will see his face in the world to come.' He said, 'Has not this man trouble enough that you should come and mock him? Can potsherds cleave together again? Is it not written, "As vessels of a potter thou shalt dash them in pieces"?' Rabbi Jose replied, 'A vessel of clay is made with water and hardened with fire, but a vessel of glass is made with fire and hardened with fire. If the former is broken can it be mended? But if the latter is broken can it not be mended?' The heretic replied, 'Yes, forasmuch as it was made by the breath (of the glass-blower).' Rabbi Jose said to him, 'Let thine ears hear what thy mouth has uttered! If this vessel which was made by the breath of mortal man can be repaired, how much more that which was made by the breath of the Holy One.'"

APPENDIX III

THE THIRD DAY

The saying in Hos. vi. 2, " on the third day he will raise us up and we shall live before him," was the source of a long tradition of Jewish exegesis connected with the Resurrection. In P.R.El. 51 there is a remarkable passage based upon this ancient exegetical tradition: " All the inhabitants of the earth shall taste of death for two days, when there will be no soul of man or beast upon the earth, as it is said, ' And they that dwelt therein shall die in like manner.' On the third day He will renew them all and revive the dead and He will establish them before Him, as it is said, ' On the Third day he will raise us up, and we shall live before Him.' "

In Genesis Rabbah 91, occurs the passage : " God never leaves the righteous longer than three days in death, as we learn from Joseph (Gen. xlii. 17), from Jonah, from Mordecai, and from David. Moreover, it says in Hos. vi. 2 : ' He will raise us up.' " A similar use of Hos. vi. 2 occurs in Sanh. 97. It is well known that the Rabbinical tradition goes back to a period before the time of Christ, and that interpretations of the Scripture which may be quoted from a Rabbi of the third century A.D. may go back to a much earlier period. Hence it is possible that the saying of Jesus was based on this traditional interpretation of Hos. vi. 2, and the presence of the third day belief in the early tradition of the Resurrection is due to the desire to furnish an exact fulfilment of the saying.

SELECT BIBLIOGRAPHY

Jackson (Dr. J. Foakes) and Lake (Prof. Kirsopp): "Beginnings of Christianity" (Vols. I and II).

Lake (Prof. Kirsopp): "The Historical Evidence for the Resurrection of Jesus Christ"; "Landmarks in the History of Early Christianity"; "The Earlier Epistles of St. Paul: their Motive and Origin."

Harnack (Dr. C. G. Adolf): "The Mission and Expansion of Christianity" (2 vols. Eng. trans.); "The Acts of the Apostles."

Loisy: "Acts."

Schweitzer (Dr. A.): "Paul and his Interpreters." A Critical History. Trans. by W. Montgomery, B.A., B.D.

Meyer (Prof. Eduard): "Ursprung und Anfänge des Christentums."

Weiss (Prof. Johannes): "Paul and Jesus."

Charles (R. H.): "Eschatology, Hebrew, Jewish, and Christian"; "The Apocrypha and Pseudepigrapha of the Old Testament."

Turner (C. H.): "Studies in Early Church History."

Streeter (Canon Burnett H.): "The Four Gospels: their Origin, Sources, and Collection into the Canon."

Cadman (W. H.): "The Last Journey of Christ to Jerusalem."

Bindley (T. H., D.D.): "The Œcumenical Documents of the Faith."

Loeb Classical Library: " The Apostolic Fathers." Trans. by Prof. Kirsopp Lake (2 vols.).

Gardner (Prof. P.): " The Religious Experience of St. Paul."

Cumont (Franz): " The Oriental Religions in Roman Paganism."

Reitzenstein (Richard): " Poimandres."

Scott (Prof. E. F.): " The Kingdom and the Messiah."

INDEX

Acts xii, 8, 21, 23f., 34, 73f., 79 f., 83 f., 105
Adoptionism, 118, 125 f., 127 f., 129
Alexandria, 84, 136
Antigonus of Socho, 10
Antioch, 85–6, 92 f., 99
Apocalyptic Jewish, 11, 16, 22, 23–4, 108, 112, 114, 128, 143 f.
Apocryphal literature, 122, 132
Apollos, 1
Apostles, 3, 31, 33 f., 41, 45, 77, 85 f., 133
Apostolic Council, 92
Apotheosis, 122, 125 f.
Arianism, 127, 136
Ascension, 42, 74
Athanasius, 129

Baptism, 42, 102, 107, 122
Barnabas, 25, 99
Bishops, 85, 105, 117, 131 f., 136

Cadman, 17 f.
Canon of Scripture, 122, 129, 132
Chalcedon, 123
Charismatic ministry, 117
Charles, Canon R. H., xi, 144
Clement of Alexandria, 121
Cornelius, the proselyte, 86
Cornelius, bishop of Rome, 133
Cumont, xi, 106
Cyprian, 123, 133

Damascus, 83, 92
Deacons, 84–5
Decius, 133
Deissmann, xi
Docetism, 42, 129

Elijah, 2, 5, 11, 12
Emperor worship, 106, 109
Ephesus, 84, 126, 129

Essenes, 82
Ethics, Jewish, 111

Fig-tree, story of, 52–3
Fourth Gospel, 1, 6, 8, 18, 34 f., 59, 84, 126, 127 f., 129 f.
Francis of Assisi, 22

Galatians, 83, 89 f.
Galilee, 3, 5, 29 f., 40 f., 45, 74 f.
Gardner, Prof. P., 106
Glossolalia, 75–6
Gnosticism, 126, 132

Haggada, 145 f.
Harnack, xii, 77, 97
Harris, Dr. Rendel, 24, 101, 128
Hebrews, 84, 97, 102
Hellenism, 11
Hellenists, 84 f., 94, 97, 102
Hermas, 125
Herod, 3, 4, 17
Hogg, Prof., 8, 47 f.
Holland, Canon Scott, 141

Ignatius, 117, 133 f.
Irenæus, 129

Jackson, Prof. Foakes, xii, 25, 74
James, the Lord's brother, 13, 81, 88, 93
Jerusalem, 4–5, 18, 23, 29, 32, 40 f., 45–6, 73 f., 92 f., 97, 118
Joan of Arc, 9, 22
John the Baptist, 1, 3, 5, 84
Joseph of Arimathea, 29, 30, 34
Judaizers, 89 f., 94
Justin Martyr, 106, 129

Lactantius, 123
Lake, Prof. Kirsopp, xii, 25, 74, 125
Lapsi, 133

Lazarus, raising of, 58 f.
Leo, Tome of, 123, 136, 140
Lightfoot, 125
Logos, 121, 126, 128 f.
Loisy, xii.
Lucian, 139

Mark, original ending of, 38-9
Messiah, 2, 12, 44, 80, 82, 101, 108-9, 112 f., 124 f., 144
Messianic Kingdom, 10-12, 23-4
Meyer, Eduard, xii
Miracle, 49 f.
Mithra, 109
Mystery cults, xii, 106 f., 108 f., 121, 124, 128, 131

Neoplatonism, 128
New Age, the, 1, 2, 3, 4, 102, 109, 114, 122
Nicæa, 82, 139
Novatian, 133 f.

Olympians, the, 106
Organization, Church, 115 f., 122, 131 f.
Origen, 43, 121
Osiris, 109

Parousia, 18, 22, 101, 111, 114
Paul, 10, 12, 20 f., 34, 75-6, 83 f., 86, 89 f., 96 f., 99 f.
Pentecost, xiii, 74 f.
Peter, 3, 4, 28, 29, 32-3, 36, 39, 77 f., 88, 93
Peter, Apocryphal Gospel of, 37
Pharisees, 10, 26, 113
Philosophy, Greek, 106, 121, 135
Pre-existence, 113, 118, 126, 127 f., 129 f., 135 f.
Prophecy, 82, 101, 109, 121
Providence, 49, 53 f.

Rabbinical literature, 14, 145 f.
Reitzenstein, xi
Resurrection:
  beliefs, 8, 9, 10, 14, 20 f.
  evidence for, 28 f.
  of Jesus, 7, 8, 10, 15 f., 23 f., 28 f.
Revelation, the book of, 105, 120, 128
Rome, 84, 94, 120, 129, 136

Sacraments, 107, 109, 122, 128
Sadducees, 13
Sanday, xi
Schweitzer, 17
Science, 57, 61, 141
Scott, Prof. E. F., 96
Septuagint, 24
Serapis, 109
Son of Man, 2, 5, 16, 18, 44, 112
Source-criticism of Acts, 75 f.
Spirit, 22, 78, 81, 102 f., 114, 129
Stephen, 25, 84-5, 92, 96
Stoic philosophy, 121, 126, 128
Strack and Billerbeck, 145
Streeter, Canon B. H., 17
Supernatural, the, 47 f.
Swete, 30
Synagogue, 118
Syncretism, 110

Talmud, 11, 145
Testimonies, the, 24, 101
Third day, the, 16, 147
Traditions, the two, 40 f.
Trinity, the, 42, 44, 135 f.
Twelve, the, 3, 85 f.

Vincent of Lerinum, 132

Wisdom literature, 11

For Product Safety Concerns and Information please contact our EU
representative GPSR@taylorandfrancis.com
Taylor & Francis Verlag GmbH, Kaufingerstraße 24, 80331 München, Germany

www.ingramcontent.com/pod-product-compliance
Lightning Source LLC
Chambersburg PA
CBHW070618300426
44113CB00010B/1580